Change of Name

Fifteenth Edition

edited by
Helen Mead

LLB LLM Solicitor

LAW & TAX

© Pearson Professional Limited 1995

ISBN 075200 1760

Published by
FT Law & Tax
21–27 Lamb's Conduit Street
London WC1N 3NJ

A Division of Pearson Professional Limited

Associated Offices
Australia, Belgium, Canada, Hong Kong, India, Japan, Luxembourg,
Singapore, Spain, USA

First published 1946
Fifteenth edition 1995

Printed in Great Britain by Hartnolls

Change of Name

Contents

For my husband Malcolm.

Preface

Sadly, due to his death, JF Josling has not been able to prepare this 15th edition of *Change of Name*. I am very pleased to have been invited to undertake the task and only hope that I have done justice to his previous 14 editions.

I view the main purposes of the book as being both to assist in drawing the reader's attention to those areas of law where a change of name may be relevant, and to act as a guide as to when formal action to evidence such a change might be advisable or necessary.

The book only touches on the several areas of law where a change of name may be relevant, and is illustrated with selected cases where appropriate. It is not meant to provide anything in the way of an expert or in depth view of any particular topic and it is assumed the reader will either already know his subject, or carry out any further research necessary.

This edition covers changes of name by individuals, the change of name by companies or business being mentioned briefly only where relevant. The appropriate sections of the Children Act 1989 and the Enrolment of Deeds (Change of Name) Regulations 1994 are included.

May I draw the reader's attention to *Halsbury's Laws of England, Statutes* and *Statutory Instruments* for further information on the names of building societies, friendly societies, industrial and provident societies, ships, street and house names, trade names and trade marks.

In the preparation of this edition, many people have given variously of their time, patience and support, provided information and allowed access to research facilities. A particular 'thank you' is due to Mark Crompton of Pattinson & Scott Solicitors Windermere; Mark Thompson of Bond Pearce Solicitors Exeter; Lyn Ayrton of Booth & Co Solicitors Leeds; William Hunt, Portcullis Pursuivant of Arms, College of Arms London; Paul Kershaw and his staff at the University of Exeter Law

Library; John Morris, formerly of the Filing and Record Department of the Central Office of the Supreme Court and JA Sweeney of Devon County Council.

The law is stated as at 1 July 1995.

Helen Mead
October 1995

Table of Cases

Table of Statutes

Table of Statutory Instruments

Chapter 1

Introduction

What is a name?

A person's name is simply a label for identification and is used both by and of a person to distinguish him from another human being. What an individual's name is at any particular time is a matter of fact rather than of law, and there is usually little difficulty in changing it if the person so requires. A person who changes his name by one of the several methods described in the following chapters can always revert to his former name by the same method as employed for the original change or by one of the alternative methods.

A person's name, which usually comprises a forename or forenames and a surname, normally accrues in regard to him at birth, and is nearly always the choice of a child's parent or parents (though foundlings may instantly be dubbed by public officials and others, often according to the time or circumstances of their discovery). Many persons will use two names in daily life or business with complete propriety, eg performing artists.

Forename

This is either a Christian name, conferred on a person by the ceremony of baptism or, if the person is not baptised, a 'given' name.

Surname

'At common law a surname is merely the name by which a person is generally known': per Lord Ormrod in *D v B (Surname: Birth Registration)* [1979] Fam 38, at p 48. It comes from the reputation of a person among others who deal with him or come within the ambit of his life and can carry as much weight as the forename, even though socially first names are increasingly used in everyday contacts.

A surname is not a matter of inheritance. Only by convention have children's surnames tended to follow that of the father, or the person appearing to be the father. Where the parents of a child are not married the child usually takes the mother's surname.

The Registration of Births and Deaths Regulations 1987 (SI No 2088) define the word 'name' as not including 'surname', and prescribe that on registration of a birth the child's surname to be entered shall be that by which at the date of registration it is intended that he shall be known, presumably by the person registering the birth, whether or not the name given happens to be also the name of one or both of the parents. Buckley J in *Re T (otherwise H) (An Infant)* [1963] Ch 238 said: '. . . a person's surname is a conventional name and forms no part of his true legal name'.

The different methods of evidencing changes of Christian and other forenames, and surnames, are set out in Chapters 2, 7, 8 and 9.

Chapter 2

Acquisition of a New Name

The general rule is that any person is entitled to change his or her name at will. Willes J in *R v Smith* (1865) 4 F & F 1099 said:

> If a man has a name which displeases him, there in nothing in law to prevent his changing it to any other he likes better, provided he can get the public to adopt and use the name he prefers.

Use and reputation

The acquisition of a new name by use and reputation is really the only way by which a change of name is effected. This method is quite sufficient, and apparently more formal methods, such as a deed poll or a statutory declaration are no more than evidence of a change and are not necessary modes of adoption. 'There is no magic in a deed poll': per Buckley J in *Re T (otherwise H) (An Infant)* [1963] Ch 238. In practice, though, most persons or agencies, eg the DSS or the Land Registry, will require some form of documentary evidence when asked to note the change. *See further* Chapter 3.

It was held by Abbott CJ in *Doe d Luscombe v Yates* (1822) 5 B & Ald 544 that:

> . . . a name assumed by the voluntary act of a young man at his outset into life, adopted by all who know him, and by which he is constantly called, becomes for all purposes . . . as much and effectually his name as if he had obtained an Act of Parliament to confer it upon him.

In this case it was a condition of an estate that the beneficiary should assume the testator's surname of Luscombe and formally evidence the change, eg by way of Act of Parliament. Before his coming of age and the vesting of the estate in him, the beneficiary was using the name Luscombe and no other, but did not obtain an Act of Parliament or a Royal Licence. It was held that this did not cause him to forfeit the estate, as he

had substantially complied with the testator's directions in that he was
using the name of Luscombe when he came into the estate.

Conscious decision

In the case of an adult, or an older child, a change of name will normally
involve a conscious decision, either to initiate the change of name
himself, informing third parties of the event, and thereafter acquiescing
in its usage, or merely to acquiesce without complaint on being called or
knowing that he is being called by the new name.

In *R v Smith* (1865) 4 F & F 1099 Mr Smith allegedly signed a false
paper in connection with his marriage, giving his name as Brownson and
signing the notice John Smith Brownson. He had taken the name
Brownson when he went to live in Lincolnshire, having previously lived
all his life at Muggington in Derbyshire. After 12 months there he
proposed marriage and gave the required notice to the registrar. Willes J
held that the question was: 'had he acquired the name of Brownson in
addition to the name of Smith?' If so, he should be (and indeed was),
acquitted.

Accidental change

Names have long been subject to alteration and development by
accidental means. A person's associates may refer to him differently after
an incident, and names can be changed through clerical error, mishearing,
misreading or misunderstanding. *See* Chapter 5 for specific requirements
on the change of a child's name.

Fraud

It has always been recognised by the common law that a person may take
any name he pleases, provided that it is not done for any fraudulent
purpose, and his use of it is not calculated to deceive and inflict financial
loss on another.

An illustration of one of the earlier cases of passing off is *Burgess v
Burgess* (1853) 3 De GM & G 896 where it was held that there was no
fraud involved when William Harding Burgess, the plaintiff's son, set
himself up in a similar business to that of his father and sold similar
products (in particular Burgess's Essence of Anchovies). This was not
acompanied by fraudulent intent since he manufactured his own essence
and sold it under his own name. He sold his own goods and not anyone
else's; he was not holding out anyone else's goods as his own. It was

merely coincidental that he had the same name as the plaintiff. *See* Chapter 3 for later cases on passing off.

In *Du Boulay v Du Boulay* (1869) LR 2 PC 430, an appeal from the Court of Appeal for the Windward Islands to the Privy Council, it was held that it was not possible to prevent the mere assumption of a patronymic name of a family by a stranger who had never before been called by that name, whatever cause of annoyance it might be to that family.

The defendant, the illegitimate son of a manumitted slave of the Du Boulay family, commenced business in 1855 under the firm name of Du Boulay & Co, and subsequently Du Boulay. Until commencement of proceedings in 1865, his right to use the name was never questioned by the family, and during this time he carried on business notoriously and publicly, this presumably being known to all the Du Boulay family living in St Lucia.

It was held that even if the action were maintainable, there must be some reasonable limit within which the family were bound to proceed.

In *Cowley v Cowley* [1901] AC 450 the Countess of Cowley, who was entitled to the privileges of peerage by virtue of marriage, obtained a divorce on the grounds of Lord Cowley's misconduct and then married a commoner. Although at that stage she lost the privileges of the peerage, it was a common practice for peeresses (not being peeresses in their own right) to retain their title on remarriage, and Lady Cowley continued to hold herself out as such. Lord Cowley did not suffer any legal wrong or damage, although the court could understand that the new Lady Cowley was not particularly happy about the situation. There was no malice involved or expressed assertion of marriage by the former Lady Cowley.

In *R v Whitmore* (1914) 10 Cr App Rep 204 Thomas James Whitmore, an undischarged bankrupt, was convicted for obtaining goods by false pretences having held himself out as H Beach and as owning and carrying on a good class of bakery in Coventry. He paid for the first order of goods but then did not pay for a larger order of goods. Lord Coleridge J, at p 205, said:

> If your name is Whitmore and not Beach, and you say it is Beach for leading people to believe it is not Whitmore then it is a false statement of fact, and in this case done with intent to defraud.

In *Clark v Chalmers* 1961 SLT 325 Jack Smart Chalmers called himself Barneston McKay on a car insurance certificate proposal form, in breach of the Road Traffic Act 1960, s 235(2)(*a*), under which it was an offence to make a false statement or withhold material information for the purpose of obtaining the issue of a certificate of insurance.

It was held by the Lord Justice-General that while in Scotland people are free to change their names:

> ... a man cannot have two names at the same time and if a man knows that his name is A and states that his name is B that statement is false. If he could show that he had abandoned one name and taken another there might be no charge but the charge is that his name, as he well knew, is Jack Smart Chalmers and the entry in the proposal form is false.

Additional surnames

The assumption of an additional surname amounts to a change. The author George Eliot assumed such an additional name after the death of George Henry Lewes in 1878, taking the name of Lewes at the end of her own name of Mary Ann Evans and evidencing the step by deed poll.

Prefixes and suffixes

A hyphenated prefix or suffix to an existing name is fairly common, and even such a simple step as the insertion of a hyphen between the last forename and the surname has the effect of changing the surname. This is the case even when the last forename and the surname consist of the same word, as where John Hall Hall is changed to John Hall-Hall. *See also* Chapter 4, pp 48–9.

Evidence

It is a matter of evidence whether a change by repute has in fact taken place. In *Davies v Lowndes* (1835) 1 Bing NC 597 it was a condition of the taking of an estate that the devisee changed his name to Selby. In the events that occurred it was not possible to say exactly when the change had taken place, but it was clear from the evidence that the new name had been acquired gradually.

See also Fendall v Goldsmid (1877) 2 PD 263 where the petitioner for nullity of a marriage had obtained a decree dissolving her marriage and subsequently remarried her husband. In the banns for the second marriage she was described by her former married name, she in the interval having been known by her maiden name. On an application to annul the second marriage it was held:

> ... marriage confers a name on a woman which becomes her actual name and she can only acquire another by reputation. The circumstances must be very exceptional to render a marriage celebrated in the actual names of the parties invalid.

If the evidence is adequate the reputed name will become effective. Thus in *R v Billingshurst (Inhabitants)* (1814) 3 M & S 250 a man was given the name Langley when born, christened Abraham, and became known as George Smith for a period of three years before marrying in that name. The marriage was held good. It would have been otherwise if the new name had been assumed for a fraudulent purpose. *See also Frankland v Nicholson* (1805) 3 M & S 260 where it was held:

> If a person has acquired a name by repute, in fact the use of the true name in banns would be an act of concealment that would not satisfy the public purposes of the statute . . . names acquired by use and reputation might supersede the use of the true name.

See also Pougett v Tomkyns (1812) 3 M & S 262*n* where a father brought an action to annul the marriage of his son to his grandmother's servant on the grounds, inter alia, of invalid publication of banns. The son's name given in baptism was William Peter Pougett, but he had always been known by the name Peter. The banns were published in the name William Pougett and the marriage contracted in the same name. It was held that 'a publication in false names is no publication'. The concealment in this case was intentional as the son had omitted to use the name by which he was normally known by his family.

There was held to be no concealment where the surname used in the publication of banns was one which the person had never borne, but was mistakenly entered on the register of baptisms. *See R v Tibshelf Inhabitants* (1830) 1 B & Ad 190 where a woman called Mary Hodgkison was called White in the publication of banns. The name White had been entered in the register of baptisms by mistake. She had never used the name and although she gave the wrong name to the clergyman for the publication of the banns she had no intention to mislead. There was 'an extreme anxiety to be right'.

Compare *Mather v Ney* (1807) 3 M & S 265*n* where it was held:

> . . . the woman, from a mere idle and romantic frolic insisted on having her banns put up in the name of Wright to which she had no sort of pretension.

See also Diddear v Faucit (1821) 3 Phillim 580 where the actress Harriet Elizabeth Diddear clandestinely married the actor John Faucit, whose real name was Savill, in defiance of her parents' wishes. The banns were published in the names of John Faucit and Harriet Diddear. She subsequently petitioned to anul the marriage on account of undue publication of banns, the objection being that John Faucit was in fact John Savill. Although the judge was not satisfied that because John Faucit was an actor that that was the name by which he was widely known, he held that there was no intention to defraud or conceal at the time of publication of the banns, and indeed the omission of the name Elizabeth from the wife's name was nothing other than accidental. *See also Wyatt v Henry* (1817) 2 Hag Con 215 and *Orme v Holloway* (1847) 5 Notes of Cases 267.

Again in *Dancer v Dancer* [1949] P 147 the reputed name of a person about to be married had, it was held, overridden her native surname so as to satisfy the Marriage Act 1823, s 7 which required the disclosure of the true Christian names and surnames in the notice to lead to the publication of banns. Section 8 of the Marriage Act 1949, replacing this section, omits the word 'true'. In this case Jessamine Knight lived with her mother and Mr Roberts for 14 years until he died, was brought up as their child, and was not told her real surname until she was 16 years old. She and her fiancé agreed, on the advice of their vicar, to publish the banns in the name of Roberts in order to avoid misleading the public. On a subsequent petition for nullity it was held that as she had consented to the publication of the surname Roberts in the banns there had been no fraudulent intentions to conceal the true facts, but rather the reverse.

Compare with *Chipchase v Chipchase* [1939] 3 All ER 895 where a decree of nullity was granted. Here the wife had given her maiden name and stated she was a widow for the publication of the banns. She had wanted to conceal the fact that she was already married. *See also* Chapter 3, pp 12–13.

Forenames and Christian names

There is no restriction on an individual's power to change his forename as well as or instead of his surname. Forenames can be acquired as additional or replacement names simply by use and reputation and without formality; or the change can be evidenced by one of the formal methods as set out in Chapters 7 and 8. A new forename may also be conferred by Royal Licence: *see* Chapter 8.

In *R v Billingshurst (Inhabitants) above* Abraham Langley validly assumed the new forename George over a period of three years.

Legal transactions

Persons are usually to be identified, even in legal transactions, by the names by which they are in fact known, irrespective of their original or baptismal names. If a person signs a document in a forename other than his true Christian name or forename, he is then bound and can be sued, and sue, as if he had signed in his true Christian name or forename.

In *Walden v Holman* (1704) 6 Mod Rep 115 the defendant, who was sued in his Christian name of Benjamin, pleaded that he was baptised in the name of John. Holt LCJ stated:

> It is not true to say that one baptised by the name of John cannot be known by another name.

In *Edward Evans v Henry King, otherwise Henry Vaughan King* (1745) Willes 554 the declaration (statement of claim relating to work and labour) described the defendant by the name of Henry King. He was subsequently attached in the name of 'Henry King, otherwise Henry Vaughan King'. The defendant pleaded that he could not be attached as the same person as against whom the proceedings were brought because he was baptised Henry Vaughan. Willes LCJ held, on the facts, that he could not be said to have two names at the same time.

In *Jones v Macquillin* (1793) 5 Term Rep 195 the defendant was baptised Richard James, but in the declaration (statement of claim) was called James Richard. It was pleaded in abatement that he had always been known as Richard James, and it was held that the misplacement of the names caused the defendant's name to be as different from his real name as if any other name had been attributed to him.

In *Gould v Barnes* (1811) 3 Taunt 504 Joseph Barnes completed a bond in the name of Thomas Barnes. He was sued in his real name of Joseph. It was held that if a person signed a bond by a wrong Christian name, and was subsequently sued on it, then he should be sued in the name in which he signed. In this case it was admitted that if he had been sued in the name of Thomas and then pleaded in abatement that his name was Joseph he would have been estopped by the bond.

In *Addis v Norris* (1831) 7 Bing 445 a deed had been executed in the name of one Patrick Power who then obtained his certificate of birth from Tenerife, his place of birth, which showed he was baptised in the name of Patricio Nicholas Placedo Power. Tindall CJ held that no alteration of the deed was necessary:

> . . . we are not to make it to humour the whims of conveyancers.

In *Williams v Bryant* (1839) LJ 85 the defendant executed a bond in the name of William Bryant. This was not his baptismal name, but one by which he was well known at the time of execution. The act performed in the assumed name was held to be good.

Christian names

A Christian name is conferred on a person of any age by the ceremony of baptism (the sacrament by which an individual is admitted into the Church of Christ) and the particulars of the Christian name or names are entered in the Register of Baptisms. It is said that a change of Christian name (including a compound baptismal name) is not normally valid. *See below* for change of a Christian name at confirmation. In *R v Smith above* Willes J observed that a man could not change his Christian name. The question was 'had he by use and reputation acquired the name of Brownson in addition' to his other names.

In *Re Richards, ex p Richards* (1842) 6 Jur 136 it was stated that it is presumed that where more than one baptismal name has been conferred on a person, he is known by the first name.

In *Re Parrott, Cox v Parrott* [1946] Ch 183 a testator directed his trustees to hold his residuary estate, subject to a life interest in the income for his widow, for Tim Harrington Spencer Cox (in the will called Tim Spencer Cox) if on attaining the age of 21 he should, inter alia, assume and take the name of Walter Tim Spencer Parrott. It was held the condition was impossible of performance and void for uncertainty, and that Tim Harrington Spencer Cox was absolutely entitled in reversion. Vaisey J referred to *Davidson's Precedents and Forms in Conveyancing* 3rd edn (1873), Part 1:

> Where the legatee is of a different Christian name from the testator he cannot of course part with his own Christian name nor can he take that of the testator except as part of a compound surname consisting of the Christian name and the surname of the testator.

Vaisey J went on to hold: 'There are only two, or at the most three, ways in which a Christian name may be legally changed', as follows:

(1) by Act of Parliament, eg Baines Name Act of 1907;

(2) by the bishop at confirmation—and this was the case of Sir Francis Gawdie, Chief Justice of the Court of Common Pleas who was baptised Thomas and confirmed Francis; and

(3) (an anomalous method) by the addition of a name on adoption.

However, as to the latter the precise quality of such a name is in doubt for no one can in strictness possess more than one Christian name whether it consists of one word or of several.

The dicta of Vaisey J met with immediate criticism (*see*, eg 111 JP News 163), and it is believed that they are widely disregarded today.

Deeds poll (*see* Chapter 7) purporting to change baptismal names are frequently executed. The Central Office of the Supreme Court will accept a deed poll purporting to change a Christian name provided the householder's declaration is endorsed with the appropriate certificate. This should state that: 'Notwithstanding the decision of Mr Justice Vaisey in the case of *Re Parrott's Will Trusts, Cox v Parrott*, the applicant desires the enrolment to proceed'. *See* Chapter 7.

The College of Arms, however, will not enrol a deed poll purporting to change a person's Christian name.

Prior to amendment by the Companies Act 1989, the legislature itself referred, in the Companies Act 1985, Sched 1, para 1(*a*) to 'any former Christian name and surname', though it must be said that it defined Christian name as including any forename. As amended, that same para 1(*a*) refers to 'present name, any former name . . .', and in the amended Sched 1, para 4(*a*) name is defined as 'a person's Christian name (or other forename) and surname . . .'

Change of Christian name at confirmation

A person's Christian name may be added to or altered at the discretion of a bishop at a confirmation ceremony, the person being confirmed in the new name which then is deemed to be the lawful Christian name. Confirmation is only concerned with Christian names. If a Christian name is changed by way of addition of a name, this will then be used in preference to the existing former name.

The bishop's discretionary power, which is said to have originated in the need for disposing of *lascivia nomina*, that is to say, names possessing some improper connotation which had been given in baptism incautiously, or had subsequently acquired such a connotation, will only be exercised in favour of a good and sufficient reason. The bishop's signed certificate of change of Christian name is recorded in the baptismal and confirmation registers.

Chapter 3

Effect of a Change of Name

A change of name carried out bona fide by any of the means described in this book is effective for all purposes in law, although differing types of evidence of the change may be acceptable for different purposes.

Marriage

Banns of marriage are published after the clergyman has been notified, inter alia, of the Christian names and surnames of the parties intending to marry.

See Pougett v Tomkyns at p 7 where it was held that in a case where the banns were called in the name of William Pougett, whereas the party's name given in baptism was William Peter Pougett and he was always known as Peter Pougett, there was a false publication.

Banns of marriage may be called in a new surname though it was acquired only by reputation. In *Diddear v Faucit above* at p 7 publication of the banns was held valid in the name of Faucit where that was the surname by which John Savill was widely known.

See Wyatt v Henry (1817) 2 Hag Con 215 where a man who had become known by a new Christian name in preference to his original one was held, on the facts, not to be able to use the new name as the true name for publication of banns; and also *Dancer v Dancer* [1949] 2 All ER 731 where Jessamine Knight correctly published banns in the surname Roberts by which she had been known since childhood. *See further* p 8 as to the facts of this case.

However, this would not necessarily be the case if the change were effected with a deceitful motive. In *Chipchase v Chipchase* at p 8 the publication of banns in a maiden name and the description of a married woman as 'widow' were to conceal an existing marriage.

See also the more modern case of *National Insurance Decision R (G) 1/68* [1968] CLY 2633 where a woman tried to claim widow's benefit under the National Insurance Act 1965 on the death of her husband. It became apparent that she, being a divorcee, had remarried without disclosing her divorce and fraudulently caused publication of the marriage banns to proceed in her maiden name. For the purposes of the Act the marriage was null and void.

A partial omission from a name has been held not to invalidate the publication of the banns in *Diddear v Faucit above.*

See also the cases mentioned in Chapter 2 at pp 6–7.

A woman usually takes her husband's surname on marriage and retains it despite divorce or anulment, or bereavement. She can, of course, retain her maiden or former surname on a first or later marriage, or abandon a married name in favour of another altogether.

Elections

The Representation of the People Act 1983 requires that the 'full' names of a candidate for election should be disclosed on nomination. Section 50 of the Act (reproducing similar provisions in earlier Acts) provides that neither a misnomer nor an inaccurate description of a person recorded on the parliamentary or local government electoral registers, or any notice, record, list or other papers necessary for the purposes of:

(a) the Act (including records and lists published under the Representation of the People Act 1985, as amended: *see* ss 6–9); or

(b) the Representation of the People Regulations 1986 (SI No 1081), as amended,

is to affect the operation of those registers or other documents where the description of the person is such as to be commonly understood.

Section 50 and the 1986 Regulations applied to European Parliamentary elections by the European Parliamentary Elections Regulations 1986 (SI No 2209), as amended.

As to the offence of personation, *see* the Representation of the People Act 1983, s 60. However, this section does not relate to someone who applies for ballot papers in a name on a register which has been entered there for the purposes of giving him a vote, but is neither his original name nor an acquired name. *See R v Fox* (1887) 16 Cox CC 166 where overseers of the register of electors mistakenly named Patrick Fox as James Cummings. He was held not guilty of personation when he proceeded to apply for the papers in that name.

For a more recent example of a case of personation *see Thompson v Dann; Re a Local Government Election for Eel Brook Electoral Division of Hammersmith and Fulham LBC* [1994] TLR 545.

In *R v Thwaites* (1853) 1 E & B 704 one Joseph Cowell had been mistakenly entered in the burgess roll as James Cowell and at an election had voted in the name of James Cowell. It was held that Cowell's vote held good, despite the incorrect description. Only the mode of voting was irregular; there was no dispute that Cowell was entitled to vote. The misnomer section (for that is all that this was) under the relevant statute then in force regularised the position: 'The right man has voted, but has voted under a wrong name'.

One can go further than this in a case where there has been a deliberate acquisition for all purposes (and not merely for the occasion) of a new or additional name. *R v Casey* [1914] 2 IR 243 concerned a candidate for election as a councillor for a rural district council. His original name was Michael Walsh but for many years he had called himself Michael B Walsh in order to distinguish himself from others in the locality who were called by the same name. He carried on all his business and private life under the style of Michael B Walsh, and this was the name in which his nomination papers were handed in. The returning officer who knew him as Michael B Walsh rejected the papers as not fully setting out the full surname and other names.

Apart from any question of correction of a misnomer (the relevant section applying here), the court was of the opinion that the paper was correct. Even if his full name were Michael Barry Walsh (Barry being his mother's name which he did not in fact use), he would be quite entitled to assume the name Michael B Walsh and had done so in this case for many years.

In *Greenway-Stanley v Paterson* [1977] 2 All ER 663 a court held that the introduction of a hyphen between a person's last Christian name and the surname on his birth certificate raised no doubt about his identity.

One born Alfred George Greenway Stanley, who hyphenated his name to read Greenway-Stanley in the late 1940s and was entered as such in the electoral roll in 1962, was elected variously as borough councillor, district councillor and mayor in the 1960s and 1970s, in that name. On then standing for re-election, the returning officer became aware, by way of anonymous letter, that the candidate still used his surname Stanley for various purposes. The nomination papers were rejected as invalid. It was held there was nothing to raise doubt about the candidate's identity as shown on the nomination papers, and even if the returning officer did have cause to make enquiries, he should have concluded that the candidate was properly described for the purposes in question. This was so particularly because he had been elected on several previous occasions in the name of Greenway-Stanley and had carried on business in that name since about 1948. There was no intent to deceive.

Cases on election law have held that persons subscribing a nomination paper are required to do so with their usual signatures, whatever form their names may take on the electoral register. *See* for example *Bowden v Besley* (1888) 21 QBD 309 where Manisty J considered the form of nomination paper which included a column headed 'signature', containing as a specimen or example merely the initials 'AB'. He read this to mean that the usual or ordinary signature of the nominator was required.

The case was applied in *Re Melton Mowbray (Egerton Ward) UDC Election* [1969] 1 QB 192 where an elector had assented to a nomination by writing 'E Marment', this being her usual signature on cheques, insurance papers, documents at work and elsewhere; whereas her name on the roll was Nellie Marment and her parents, workmates and friends addressed her as Nellie. Her husband had entered her on the electoral roll as Nellie as that was the name by which she was commonly known.

The Divisional Court held that the returning officer had wrongly rejected the paper. Under the relevant rule (the UDC Election Rules 1951, r 6), an assentor to a nomination should sign by their usual signature, and not a signature reflecting the full name or name as recorded on the electoral register. Paull J held that signing 'Nellie Marment' might be contrary to the law on technical grounds, and it was quite clear that the signature was that of 'Marment, Nellie', on the register.

In the recent case of *Sanders v Chichester* [1994] TLR 620, a candidate for an election to the European Parliament described himself as a Literal Democrat. There was also a Liberal Democrat candidate who narrowly missed being elected. It was held that under r 6(2) of the Parliamentary election rules (as set out in the Representation of the People Act 1983, Sched 1), that although the candidate's full names and home address must be set out in the nomination papers, a description is not obligatory and, if given, need only be sufficient to enable the candidate to be identified. Any confusion on the part of the voters was not relevant for the purposes of the Act and the rules unless the description cast doubt upon the candidate's identification provided by the full name and address.

For alteration to electors' lists and the electoral register *see* the Representation of the People Regulations 1986 (SI No 1081), reg 37(2) and the Representation of the People Act 1983, s 11(1).

Passports

General

The normal practice of the United Kingdom Passport Agency (an executive agency of the Home Office) where a change of name is involved is as set out *below* (subject to consideration of exceptional individual cases).

An applicant for a passport who has changed his or her name otherwise than by marriage or on adoption, must produce evidence that the change has been made for all purposes, eg a change of name deed or statutory declaration. This is also applicable in the case of a child whose name has changed if the child is to be included in the applicant's own passport. Marriage, divorce and adoption certificates will be required where relevant.

In a case where satisfactory evidence of the assumption for all purposes of the new name is not produced, an observation recording the change of name is entered on the observations' page of the passport, eg 'Holder's name was formerly John William Brown'.

Clearly, where it is proposed to change a name and there is any likelihood of the individual requiring passport facilities, it is sensible that approval of the desired form is obtained from the Passport Office in advance, if possible, in order to avoid any delay caused by a change in policy.

The evidence may take various forms, eg:

(a) a deed poll, whether enrolled or not;

(b) a notarial instrument;

(c) a certificate from the court of the Lord Lyon of Scotland;

(d) a certificate of record in the Books of Council and Session in Scotland;

(e) a certificate of record at the College of Arms;

(f) a birth certificate issued under the Registration of Births, Deaths and Marriages (Scotland) Act 1965, s 43;

(g) an advertisement in the press;

(h) a marriage certificate recording both the old and the new names of the bridegroom;

(i) a certificate of naturalisation in which both the new and former names of the applicant appear;

(j) a statutory declaration setting out the full circumstances;

(k) a special Act of Parliament (a very rare case, *see* p 110); or

(l) a letter from a responsible person (such as a medical practitioner or minister of religion) who has known the applicant in both names, and can testify that the change has been made for all purposes.

Standard ten-year passport

Form A is applicable for those aged 16 or over (anyone who has attained the age of 16 *must* have their own passport), and requires a change of name, other than by adoption, to be recorded in Sections 2 (the applicant) and 5 (children to be included). Those who wish to travel immediately after changing their name on marriage must apply on Form PD2 for a passport in the future married name.

Visitor's passport

Home Office Form VP lists documents acceptable as evidence of eligibility, and requires certain of them to be in the 'present' name of the applicant. The form does not list submission of evidence of a change of name as a requirement, nor is there any space in the form for insertion of a former name as compared with the Form A for the standard ten-year passport.

A Visitor's passport cannot be issued in a future married name for use immediately after marriage. Nor can the passport be altered at all after issue. Evidence of change during the validity should be kept with the passport, or application made for a fresh passport.

Children

As long as no objection has been lodged by a parent or other objector at a United Kingdom passport office, normal passport facilities are usually granted to children.

A child who has attained the age of eight may hold a British Visitor's passport which is valid for one year only. Children who have attained the age of 16 must have their own passport, whether a standard ten-year one or Visitor's, but those aged up to 16 can be included in the passport (standard ten-year or Visitor's) of their parent, step-parent, adoptive parent, brother or sister. Form B must be used for a separate passport for a child under age 16.

A parent or guardian must grant consent for inclusion on a passport (even where the child is to be included on another relative's passport) or the issue of any passport to a child who has not attained the age of 18 (unless married or in HM forces). An exception to this rule is, where the parents have not been married to each other the mother must give the consent, unless the father has been awarded parental responsibility. Production of the marriage certificate for a married child will be required.

Where an old custody order or a present residence order exists, then the person awarded custody or in whose favour the residence order has been made must sign the consent form on the application form.

The child's name will normally be that by which he or she is currently known for all purposes.

In cases where the parents' consent to the issue of a passport in a child's new name is not forthcoming, a passport may be issued in the new name with an endorsement on the observations' page that the holder is also known as (the original name).

The United Kingdom Passport Agency has issued guidance on the issue of passports for and including children, and deals with objections to the issue of such passports if a UK court has made one of a number of orders, eg a residence order or an old custody, or care and control order. *See* Chapter 5.

Registered land

See generally the *Encyclopaedia of Forms & Precedents* 5th edn (Butterworth & Co), vol 25, and more specifically the Land Registration Rules 1925 (SI No 1093), r 249, under which the Registrar may from time to time make any formal alterations in the register as to any change of name, etc of any proprietor or otherwise as he may deem proper.

Evidence of identity is not normally submitted to the Land Registry on an application for the registration of a disposition. However, on the making of a disposition of registered land any change should be referred to and evidence of the change submitted with the application. The Land Registry will accept a marriage certificate, in the case of marriage, and in other cases an enrolled or unenrolled deed poll, a copy of an advertisement in the *London Gazette*, or a statutory declaration. Depending on whether or not the document submitted is an original or a certified copy, the Land Registry will make its own copy for retention, returning the original, or retain the copy submitted.

Again it is clearly sensible to clarify with the appropriate Land Registry (if possible in advance of the completion of a disposition) whether an existing or proposed document recording the change of name is acceptable. The Land Registry will deal with each case on its own merits in the light of the surrounding circumstances.

By virtue of the Land Registration Rules 1925 (SI No 1093), r 249 the Registrar has power to alter the registers to reflect any change in the name of the proprietor or otherwise, and by virtue of r 13, if any clerical error is discovered in a register the Registrar (subject to appeal to the court) again has power to make a correction if it can be done without affecting a registered interest. He may give notices and require evidence such as he thinks fit. For forms *see Court Forms in Civil Proceedings* 2nd edn (Butterworth & Co 1993), vol 23, pp 608–618.

On an application for a first registration, the Land Registration Rules 1925, r 20 provide that the application must be accompanied by all such original deeds and documents relating to the title as the applicant has in his possession or under his control. Any person purchasing an unregistered property which will require first registration will be well advised to satisfy themselves as to the adequacy of evidence of any change of name of estate owners and mortgagees in the title prior to exchange of contract: *see* land charges *below*. *See* r 86 as to alterations in instruments after delivery for registration.

Land charges

Again *see generally* the *Encyclopaedia of Forms & Precedents* 5th edn (Butterworth & Co), vol 25.

Unregistered land searches should be made against all names of all those named in the documentation as having been estate owners from the commencement date of the root of title.

It is clearly essential to search against every alternative name in which a charge may have been registered and particular attention should be given to the name combinations of hyphenated or prefixed names or a name composed of two or more names, as the Land Charges Registry will search against the names exactly as stated in the application.

In any case of doubt enquiry should be made of the Land Charges Registry as to how it would search against a particular name or combination of names, eg abbreviations of surnames will be searched only as written on the application, not in full.

In *Oak Co-operative Building Society v Blackburn* [1968] Ch 730 registration against a name then in use by the estate owner was held valid despite the fact that it differed from the name on his birth certificate. The registration was in the name of Frank but the correct name of the estate owner was Francis.

The facts were that, in 1958, Phyllis Cairns contracted to purchase a property from the owner, an estate agent trading as Frank D Blackburn, and entered into possession. The agent's real name was Francis David Blackburn.

A mortgage by Blackburn was registered in the name of Francis David Blackburn. Cairns registered an estate contract in the name of Frank David Blackburn.

In connection with a second charge, the Oak Co-operative Building Society subsequently obtained a clear search against Francis David Blackburn and, relying on it, advanced monies to him on the security of the property. In an appeal on a subsequent possession action by the Society, it was held that Cairns's registration in the slightly inaccurate name was not a nullity. Although it would not be enforceable against a person who obtained a clear search against Blackburn's correct names, it was effective as against a person who did not apply for an official search, or if they did, who did so in an incorrect name.

However, where a Class F charge had been registered against Erskine Alleyne instead of Erskine Owen Alleyne (the latter being the name by which the estate owner was described in the deeds relating to the property), it was held that this was a misregistration. An official certificate of search which omitted mention of the charge was held to be conclusive under the Land Charges Act 1925, s 17(3), so that the Class F charge did not take precedence over a first charge to the Greater London Council which was protected by the certificate. The birth certificate of the estate owner bore no baptismal name at all in this case: *see Diligent Finance Co Ltd v Alleyne* (1971) 23 P & CR 346.

In dealing with titles and estates of deceased persons, in addition to searching against the deceased and the personal representatives, a search may also be carried out against the President of the Family Division of the High Court. *See also* the Law of Property (Miscellaneous Provisions) Act 1994, Pt II, by virtue of which the Public Trustee assumes the President's functions. *See also* for reference the Public Trustee (Notices Affecting Land) (Title on Death) Regulations 1995 (SI No 1330), in force as from 1 July 1995.

Wills and probate

If a beneficiary has changed his name then that, on its own account, should not affect his right to receive any benefit under the terms of a will.

When making application for a grant of representation the deceased's full true name should be shown in the oath and, additionally, any alias if he made a will or held property in that alias. *See* the Non-Contentious Probate Rules 1987 (SI No 2024), r 9.

Stamp duty

Deeds poll dated before 26 March 1985 were subject to a stamp duty of 50 pence (formerly ten shillings). The duty was then abolished: *see* the Finance Act 1985, s 85(1) applying to instruments executed on or after 26 March 1985 and instruments executed on or after 19 March 1985 but not stamped before 26 March 1985. An unenrolled deed poll bearing a date before that mentioned, and not duly stamped in accordance with the law in force at the time when it was first executed, is not receivable in evidence in civil proceedings except under penalty, nor available for any purpose whatever: *see* the Stamp Act 1891, s 14. It will, however, be receivable in criminal proceedings and a witness may be allowed to refer to an unstamped deed poll in order to jog his memory.

Court and tribunal proceedings

A person may sue and be sued by a name that he has acquired by any of the means described in this book, but his rights and obligations acquired or undertaken before the change are not affected in any way.

Supreme Court

A Chancery Division *Practice Direction (Ch D) (Applications and Change of Name) (No 1 of 1984)* [1984] 1 WLR 447 requires a change of name in proceedings to be notified promptly to all other parties, and the new name substituted in all future proceedings in the action, mentioning the former name in brackets.

In the following paragraphs references to notes are to those contained in *The Supreme Court Practice 1995* (Sweet & Maxwell).

The Rules of the Supreme Court 1965 (SI No 1776) ('RSC') dealing with the writ of summons state in Ord 6(1) that every writ must be in Form No 1 in Appendix A. The note to this Order refers readers to Ord 15, r 7 and its appended note on marriage, and *Practice Direction (Queen's Bench: 17(4))* Vol 2, part 3A, para 730 for the practice on the change of name of a female party on marriage.

See RSC Ord 15, r 6 as to misjoinder of parties. RSC Ord 15, r 7 deals with a change of parties by reason of death, etc.

In the note appended thereto on marriage it is stated that where a female party changes her name on marriage then, in Queen's Bench Division actions, written notice must be filed in the Action Department of the Central Office or the appropriate District Registry, the other party or parties to the proceedings being served with a copy. The new surname will be substituted and the former surname shown in brackets for further proceedings. *See Practice Direction (Queen's Bench 17(4)) above.*

Where a party seeks to have the name of another (female) party changed in the proceedings, believing her to have married, the application should be made by way of summons, unless otherwise directed.

Amendment to documents in proceedings may be made with or without leave.

RSC Ord 20 deals with the court's discretion to allow amendment of proceedings, including correction of a party's name. Order 20, r 1 which deals with amendment of a writ without leave applies, inter alia, to amendments to correct only unintentional mistakes, errors or omissions, eg where a party's name has been wrongly spelt or a clarifying description is required (eg married woman), provided the identity of the party is the same. The note to Ord 20, r 1 states that the writ and statement of claim should show the same names of parties and a mere misnomer may be corrected. *Whittam v WJ Daniel & Co Ltd* [1962] 1 QB 271 is cited as an example of a case regarding a mere misnomer.

Note that there is no obligation on the court to allow the amendment. The court *may* 'allow the plaintiff to amend his pleadings . . . on such terms. . . as may be just and in such manner (if any) as it may direct'. It is clearly essential to take care to cite the parties' names correctly at the outset.

See RSC Ord 20, r 2 as to amendment of the acknowledgment of service and Ord 20, r 3 which deals with amendment of the pleadings without leave. RSC Ord 20, r 5 deals with amendment of the writ and pleadings with the leave of the court. The note to Ord 20, r 5 states that the court has a discretion to allow an amendment to correct the style of a party's name even after the expiry of any limitation period and even if it is alleged that the effect is to substitute a new party.

However, there must have been a genuine mistake originally, and be no doubt as to the identity of the person intending to sue or be sued: *see,* eg *Evans Construction Co Ltd v Charrington & Co Ltd and Bass Holdings Ltd* [1983] QB 810, where there was a mistake as to the defendant. The solicitor for Evans Construction Co Ltd mistakenly named Charrington & Co Ltd (assignee of the reversion to a seven-year lease, and managing agent for Bass Holdings Ltd on the grant of a new supplemental lease to the plaintiff) as landlord in an originating application in connection with an application for a new tenancy under the Landlord and Tenant Act 1954, s 29(3). The solicitor should have named Bass Holdings Ltd, as the original landlord. A fresh application naming Bass could not be made as it would be out of time under s 29(3). It was held that the solicitor genuinely intended to sue the correct landlord under the Landlord and Tenant Act 1954, and the amendment was allowed. Order 20, r 5(3) is designed to correct a situation where B is mistakenly described as A and A is sued. It is not to be used to correct a situation where A is sued in the mistaken belief that A should be sued when in fact it is B who should be sued.

Adequate evidence of the mistake must be produced to the court, which must also be satisfied that the mistake did not mislead or cause any reasonable doubt as to the defendant's identity. It must be just for the court to permit the amendment: *see also Rodriguez v RJ Parker* [1967] 1 QB 116, and *Mitchell v Harris Engineering Co Ltd* [1967] 2 QB 703 referred to in the judgment.

In *Singh v Atombrook Ltd* [1989] 1 WLR 810 it was held that an amendment would be allowed to change the name of the defendant from Sterling Travel to Atombrook Ltd even after a final default judgment had been issued. Although the travel agency used by the plaintiff was called Sterling Travel, there was no such legal identity and it was in fact owned by Atombrook Ltd. The proceedings were not invalidated as there was no real doubt that Atombrook were the party that Singh intended to sue.

In *Thistle Hotels Ltd v Sir Robert McAlpine & Sons Ltd* (1989) *The Times*, 11 April, CA where Ord 20, r 5 applied, a writ was issued in the name of Thistle Hotels when it should have been issued in the name of Scottish and Newcastle Breweries Ltd. The two companies were connected but the properties in question were owned by the latter who were employers on contracts for building. The plaintiff was wrongly styled in the proceedings and the judge exercised his discretion in favour of the plaintiff. The mistake of fact was known to the defendant company, their insurers and solicitors, and it could not be said that they were misled.

See also The 'Sardinia Sulcis' and 'Al Tawwab' [1991] Lloyd's Law Reports 201 where a writ was issued in 1981 by charterers of the *Sardinia Sulcis* in the name of its owners, in an attempt to recover the cost of damage repairs caused by the *Al Tawwab* during the course of a lightening operation. It became apparent that the owners of the *Sardinia Sulcis* ceased to exist in 1980, and the defendants sought an order to strike out the action on the ground that it had been issued in the wrong name, or alternatively that the plaintiff was non-existent at the date of issue of the writ.

It was held that the solicitors to the charterers were genuinely mistaken as to in whom the right to sue was vested at the date of issue of the writ (the effect of a merger in Italian law meant the owner of the *Sardinia Sulcis* had ceased to exist), and the defendants were not misled in any way. Order 20, r 5(3) could be applied even though a new name and a separate legal entity were substituted, and there was no reasonable doubt as to the identity of the person intending to sue—namely the person vested with rights of ownership as at the date of issue of the writ. It was a mistake only as to a name and not to identity.

See also as to misnomer of a plaintiff the case mentioned in the note to the Order: *Alexander Mountain & Co v Rumere Ltd* [1948] 2 KB 436, CA.

County courts

The County Courts Act 1984, s 76 deals with the application of High Court practice to matters arising in county court actions. Unless otherwise provided, the general principles of practice of the High Court may be adopted and applied to county court proceedings. In the following paragraphs references to notes are to those contained in *The County Court Practice 1995* (Butterworth & Co).

The note to s 76 states that this application refers to guiding rules but not specific directions. Dillon LJ, in *Rolph v Zolan* [1993] 4 All ER 202, said:

> . . . that section is primarily directed to extending the powers of the county court where the county court rules make no express provision—not to curtailing express provisions in the County Court Rules.

This was a case involving service of a county court summons outside the jurisdiction, where the question was whether the scope of the County Court Rules 1981 (SI No 1687) ('CCR') Ord 7, rr 1 and 10 could be limited to service on a defendant within the jurisdiction by analogy to RSC Ord 10, r 1.

Even apart from s 76, county courts have their own wide inherent jurisdiction to regulate their own procedures and can issue their own practice directions: *see* CCR Ord 50, r 1, under which the Lord Chancellor may issue directions for the purposes of obtaining uniformity throughout the county courts.

See the note to CCR Ord 5, r 2 as to change of name by a company. The note to CCR Ord 5, r 2 also reflects the position under RSC Ord 15 *above* that if a female party changes her surname on marriage during the action the new name should be substituted for the former, that then being shown in brackets in the title to the proceedings: *Practice Direction (Supreme Court) No 13(4)*. However, if she does not take her husband's name then she should continue to be styled by her maiden name or other surname.

Under CCR Ord 15, r 1 the court has a discretion to allow, by order, amendment of proceedings to include the correction of a party's name: *see Thistle Hotels above.*

Generally, trivial errors, eg an incorrectly spelt name, can be corrected under CCR Ord 15, r 5 which is headed 'clerical mistakes in judgments or orders or errors arising therein from any accidental slip or omission'. This rule is called the slip rule and corresponds to RSC Ord 20, r 11, whereas more serious mistakes are corrected under CCR Ord 15, r 1, provided the mistake is genuine and has not misled any other person: *see* the cases listed in the note to Ord 15, r 1. *See* CCR Ord 15, r 2 for the procedure whereby a party may, without an order, amend any pleading (stated in the note to the section to include an originating application).

See also the Court Fund Rules 1987 (SI No 821), r 41 for the procedure where a person who is entitled to payment out of monies in court changes his name or style before the fund is paid, transferred or delivered to him.

Application of the CCR to business names

See also p 41 *below.* CCR Ord 5, r 9 states that any two or more persons may sue or be sued in the name of the firm in which they were partners when the cause of action arose.

The Business Names Act 1985 provides for restrictions on the names under which a person may trade and provides that names must be disclosed in business transactions. Failure to comply is a criminal offence. *See* s 1 of the Act for permitted styles of business name for individuals.

CCR Ord 5, r 10 deals with the case of a defendant carrying on business in another name. An individual may be sued, but apparently cannot sue, in a business name: *see Mason & Son v Mogridge* (1892) 8 TLR 805, referred to in the note to the Order.

If carrying on business in a name other than his own name, in England and Wales, a person may, even if he is out of the jurisdiction, be sued:

(a) in his own name followed by the words 'trading as AB'; or

(b) in his business name followed by the words (a trading name).

Family Court

See the Family Proceedings Rules 1991 (SI No 1247) and *The Family Court Practice 1995* (Jordan & Sons). Any procedural matter not provided for in the Rules is covered by the Family Proceedings Rules 1991, r 1.3 which states that, subject to the provisions of these Rules and of any enactment, the CCR and the RSC shall apply with the necessary modifications to family proceedings in a county court and the High Court respectively.

See the Family Proceedings Courts (Children Act 1989) Rules 1991 (SI No 1395), r 19 as to amendment of documents filed or served in proceedings.

Crime

See generally Blackstone's Criminal Practice 5th edn (1995).

Although anyone named in an indictment ought to be described by his forenames and surname, the Indictment Rules 1971 (SI No 1253), r 8 states that, so long as an incorrectly named person is identified reasonably precisely and the parties in the action are not misled, then any error in setting out the names will not make the proceedings invalid.

Industrial tribunals and Employment Appeal Tribunal

The Divisional Court has recently held that although an industrial tribunal is not a court of record, it is a court (*Peach Grey & Co v Sommers* [1995] IRLR 363. Its procedure is governed by the Industrial Tribunals (Constitution and Rules of Procedure) Regulations 1993 (SI No 2687).

See Sched 1, r 11(1) whereby a tribunal decision may be reviewed, inter alia, on the ground of error and r 13(1) under which the tribunal has power to regulate its own procedure. This may be relied upon for instances not specifically dealt with by any other rule. It can be used in connection with amending an originating application, or adding or substituting a respondent.

See also Sched 1, r 17 and *Watts v Seven Kings Motor Co Ltd* [1983] ICR 135 where the applicant, having been awarded compensation for unfair dismissal, discovered that Seven Kings Motor Co Ltd (which was insolvent), had not been involved in the matter at all. It was held, applying *Cocking v Sandhurst (Stationers) Ltd* [1974] ICR 650, that an Alan Reynolds, trading as Seven Kings Motor Co, should be substituted for the original respondent. In *Cocking*, p 657, Sir John Donaldson laid down a set of principles, the following being particularly relevant in the instant case:

> In deciding whether or not to exercise their discretion to allow an amendment which will add or substitute a new party, the tribunal should only do so if they are satisfied that the mistake sought to be corrected was a genuine mistake and was not misleading or such as to cause reasonable doubt as to the identity of the person intending to claim or, as the case may be, to be claimed against.

See also the Employment Appeal Tribunal Rules 1993 (SI No 2854), r 18 as to joinder of parties and r 33 as to correction of errors in the Employment Appeal Tribunal. Note the consolidating Industrial Tribunals Act 1995, due to come into force in January 1996, which deals with procedure in the industrial tribunal and Employment Appeal Tribunal.

Change of name of employer

By virtue of the Employment Protection Consolidation Act 1978 ('EP(C)A'), s 1 an employer must give a written statement of employment particulars to an employee, which must contain, inter alia, the employer's name: EP(C)A, s 1(2). There is a further duty under EP(C)A, s 4 to give the employee a written statement of any change in the information.

See further EP(C)A Pt 1, Employment Particulars, and note that as from 6 February 1995 those employees working any number of hours per week have the same statutory employment rights as full-time workers: Employment Protection (Part-time Employees) Regulations 1995 (SI No 31).

Passing off

There is no right of absolute property in a name, so that where a name has been used without fraudulent intention, no action will lie for an injunction restraining its non-commercial use: *Cowley v Cowley* [1901] AC 450; *see* particularly per Lord Lindley at p 460. Here the divorced wife of Earl Cowley continued to call herself Countess Cowley, but the court refused Lord Cowley an injunction. There was no suggestion by Lady Cowley that she was still married to Lord Cowley, or that she was entitled to a dignity. *See further* as to this case p 5.

In *Conan Doyle v London Mystery Magazine Ltd* (1949) 66 RPC 312 Sir Arthur Conan Doyle's executor brought a passing off action to restrain the defendant using the name 'Sherlock Holmes' in their magazine without clearly publicising that their business or magazine had no connection with Conan Doyle or his literary works. It was held that there was no right of property to be protected except the goodwill vested in Conan Doyle's executor (the plaintiff) in the actual stories relating to Sherlock Holmes. The defendants were not doing anything to impinge on that property right.

However, English law does recognise the right to use a particular name exclusively for trade and an infringer may be restrained by injunction: *see Du Boulay v Du Boulay* (1869) LR 2 PC 430, per Lord Phillimore:

> The right to the exclusive use of a name in connection with a trade or business is familiar to our law; and any person using that name, after a relative right of this description has been acquired by another, is considered to have been guilty of a fraud or, at least, of an invasion of another's right and renders himself liable to an action or he may be restrained from the use of the name by injunction.

Here, however, there was only annoyance caused by the assumption by a third party of a patronymic name of a large and well-known family. *See further* as to this case p 5.

In *Poiret v Jules Poiret Ltd and AF Nash* (1920) 37 RPC 177 an injunction was granted to prevent Nash using the name Poiret either on its own or together with the name Jules. The plaintiff was well known as a costumier and ladies' dress designer in Paris, exhibiting in London with many customers there. He claimed an injunction to prevent Nash (calling himself Jules Poiret and subsequently Jules Poiret & Co Ltd) trading (using the name Poiret in connection with the making and sale of ladies dresses and costumes in London) as a costumier and ladies' dressmaker. He argued that confusion in the trade and among private customers would have resulted if Paul Poiret had opened a business in London.

It was held that Nash took Poiret's name knowing that it was well respected in the dressmaking business in both London and Paris, and that his purpose had been to acquire some benefit from it for himself. Paul Poiret was entitled to protect his dresses, costumes and his reputation in England notwithstanding he had no place of business there. He was entitled to open a branch in England, to trade and make use of his established reputation in the English market without the defendant's interference and continued use of the name causing serious damage.

However, in *Levy v Walker* (1879) 10 Ch 436 the court would not interfere. The Misses Charbonnel and Walker began business in London as Parisian confectioners and bonbon manufacturers under a firm name Charbonnel & Walker.

On a dissolution Walker purchased the business and continued to trade under the style of Charbonnel & Walker. The sale of the goodwill and the business conveyed to her the right to the use of the partnership name as a description of the articles sold in that trade. That right was exclusive as against all persons so that no one else could hold himself out as carrying on the same business.

Charbonnel married Levy and they set up a similar business in Paris, trading as Charbonnel et Cie. They brought an action against Walker.

Jessel MR held that there was no threat to the Levys of liability in connection with Walker's business being carried on in England. They were not partners in Charbonnel & Walker, and notice had been given to all those who dealt with the firm at the time of the dissolution.

Walker could use the trade name unless someone else had a title to prevent her. The Levys had no such right. They were neither in London nor was any trade mark of theirs being interfered with. Charbonnel & Walker in London was not representing itself as carrying on a business of Charbonnel et Cie in Paris.

In *Joseph Rodgers & Sons Ltd v WN Rodgers & Co* (1924) 41 RPC 277 Joseph Rodgers & Sons, very well known cutlers in Sheffield, sought an injunction to prevent the defendants, also cutlers, from trading as WN Rodgers & Co or under any name of which the word Rodgers formed a part. The word Rodgers used by itself in the cutlery trade was identified with the plaintiffs.

The defendants argued that the name WN Rodgers was that of the defendant Wilfred Newbound Rodgers, that he was a skilled cutler and entitled to trade under his own name, and to mark his goods with the name WN Rodgers & Co.

The question of fact to be determined was whether what the defendants were doing was calculated to lead to the belief that they were in some way connected with the plaintiffs' firm, or that they were selling the plaintiffs' goods.

The defendant was not carrying on business under his own name but under the name WN Rodgers, and this name was much more likely to cause confusion than would be the name Wilfred Newbound Rodgers by itself.

It was held that he was entitled to carry on business under his ordinary name and that the plaintiffs were entitled to injunctions restraining him from:

    (a) carrying on a cutlery business under the name WN Rodgers & Co;

    (b) trading under any name of which the word Rodgers formed part without clearly distinguishing his business from the plaintiffs' business;

    (c) marking his cutlery with the words WN Rodgers & Co;

    (d) selling and offering for sale cutlery under the name of WN Rodgers & Co or any name of which the word Rodgers formed part without clearly distinguishing such goods from the plaintiffs goods.

The court referred to *Turton v Turton* (1889) 42 Ch D 128 where it was held the court cannot stop a man from carrying on business in his own name, although it may be the name of a better-known manufacturer, when he does nothing at all in any way to try and represent that he is that better-known and successful manufacturer.

However, this exception, it is said, is one which only authorises the use by a man of his own name—not an exception which entitles a man to make use of something which is not his own name, ie in combination with something else.

Rodgers was not carrying on business under his own name—he combined it with '& Co'; this did not come within the well-recognised exception.

A case to similar effect is *Hall of Arts and Sciences Corporation v Hall* (1934) 50 TLR 518 where the plaintiff, commonly known as The Albert Hall, tried to prevent Albert Edward Hall, an orchestra conductor, from using his business name of Albert Hall Orchestra in such a way as to mislead the public into believing there was a connection between them.

Hall argued that he had always been known as Albert Hall, and was entitled to use, and was honestly using, that name for his own business.

There were halls of the same name in other towns and indeed the plaintiffs had no orchestra.

Clauson J believed Hall was entirely in good faith, that he had previously used the name Albert Hall Orchestra in other cities, and that his business could not impinge upon that of the plaintiffs as theirs was of a quite different nature.

In *Street v Union Bank of Spain & England* (1885) 30 Ch D 156 the use of a plaintiff's personal name in the defendant's telegraphic address was not sufficient to justify an injunction to restrain the defendant from using it as such.

Edmund Street and George Jackson, advertising agents, traded as Street & Co at Cornhill and at a branch office at Carey Street, London, and were well known abroad as 'Street London'. They produced evidence alleging that they were exposed to loss and liability, and their customers had suffered damage on account of telegrams having been sent to the Union Bank. They requested an injunction to prevent the Bank from using the telegraphic address, and representing they were trading as 'Street London', or using that name in connection with their business.

The injunction was refused on the basis that neither Street, nor Street London were the name and address of the plaintiffs' firm. The Bank did not represent itself as carrying on the plaintiffs' business which was of quite a different nature to its own, nor was it attempting to acquire it.

The question whether the dictum of Romer J in the *Rodgers* case *above* was not too widely expressed was left open by the Court of Appeal in *Baume & Co v AH Moore* [1958] Ch 907 (and apparently, too, by the majority of the House of Lords in *Parker-Knoll Ltd v Knoll International Ltd* [1962] RPC 265 (*see below*)).

Certainly these cases show that if even the true name of a manufacturer is applied to his products in a manner reasonably calculated to cause confusion with those of another, an action for passing off of goods may succeed against him without proof of an intention to deceive.

In *Baume*, Romer J recited the proposition in the *Rodgers* case that:

> ... no man is entitled to carry on his business in such a way as to represent that it is the business of another ... [to which there is an exception] ... a man is entitled to carry on his business in his own name so long as he does not do anything more than that to cause confusion with the business of another and so long as he does it honestly.

Romer J said that the exception to this rule may have been expressed too widely.

However, on the facts of the *Baume* case it was the second rule in the *Rodgers* case which was relevant, ie 'that no man is entitled to describe or mark his goods as to represent that the goods are the goods of another'.

In this case, which involved the marking of goods as opposed to carrying on business, the plaintiffs, who sold watches under the registered trade mark of Baume, sought by way of a passing off action to restrain the sale by the defendants of watches carrying the mark Baume and Mercier Geneve, and to prevent infringement of their trade mark.

Romer J said there was no exception to that second rule. It was no defence that there was no intention to deceive. A true statement which carried a false representation leading others to believe that the watches were the plaintiffs' would warrant an injunction.

Use of same names is strong evidence of the intent to deceive, but even if there is no deception a person will be restrained from using the name in question if he does not act to prevent misunderstanding occurring. Innocent and honest user does not avail as a defence in a passing off action. The conclusion in the *Baume* case was that there was a reasonable chance of confusion and a real probability of association with the plaintiffs' goods.

As to infringement of the trade mark, there was a different conclusion: the defendants were in breach of the Trade Marks Act 1938, s 4 in that they had incorporated the whole of the plaintiffs' mark in their own. However, s 8 of the Act provided protection as the use of the name was bona fide.

In *Parker-Knoll Ltd v Knoll International Ltd* [1962] RPC 265 there were again actions for both infringement of a trade mark and passing off.

The House of Lords upheld the Court of Appeal in that:

  (a) there should be an injunction to restrain infringement of the trade mark provided that the defendants' bona fide use of their full name Knoll International, with or without the word Limited as provided by the Trade Marks Act 1938, s 8, must not be fettered;

  (b) the defendants should be restrained from passing off by their use of the words Knoll and Knoll International, but this should be qualified by the words 'without clearly distinguishing their goods from the goods of the plaintiffs'.

Lord Denning dissenting said that the injunction to restrain passing off should not extend to the use of the full name of the defendants, and considered that the law of passing off does not interfere with any bona fide use by a person of his own name, whether as a trading name or trade mark, so long as he does not do anything more than that to cause confusion. He would not draw 'the illogical and incongruous distinction beween trade marks and passing-off' which was drawn by the Court of

Appeal in the *Baume* case. He held that the defendants were honestly entitled to use their own name Knoll International with or without the word Limited but were not entitled to abbreviate it to Knoll only.

Lord Morris of Borthy-Gest set out propositions which he thought applied to such a case:

(1) No one has the right to represent his goods as being the goods of someone else (*Reddaway v Banham* [1896] AC 199; *Joseph Rodgers & Sons Limited v WN Rodgers & Company* (1924) 41 RPC 277).

(2) The court will restrain the making of any such representation even though it is not made fraudulently (see *John Brinsmead & Sons Limited v Brinsmead* (1913) 30 RPC 493) . . .

(3) A name may be used as a mark under which a person's goods are sold so that the name comes to denote goods made by that person and not the goods made by anyone else or even made by anyone else who has the same name. So also a mark under which a person's goods are sold may come to denote goods made by that person. The name or the mark will have acquired a secondary meaning (see *Chivers v Chivers* (1900) 17 RPC 420).

(4) It follows that someone may, even by using his own name, and using it innocently, make a representation that is untrue, that is a representation that goods which are in fact his own are the goods of someone else (see *Reddaway v Banham* [1896] AC 199).

He cited the principle in the *Rodgers* case that 'no man is entitled so to describe or mark his goods as to represent that the goods are the goods of another and that to the rule as so stated there is no exception at all . . .'

(5) It is a question of fact . . . whether . . . a name or a mark has acquired a secondary meaning so that it denotes or has come to mean goods made by a particular person and not goods made by any other person even though such other person may have the same name.

(6) If it is proved that . . . a name or mark has acquired a secondary meaning then it is a question for the court whether a defendant whatever may be his intention, is so describing his goods that there is a likelihood that a substantial section of the purchasing public will be misled into believing that his goods are the goods of the plaintiff (see *Chivers & Sons v S Chivers & Co Limited* (1900) 17 RPC 420).

He concluded that the likelihood of the sale of Knoll or Knoll International furniture being a deception (however innocent) was established. He agreed with the Court of Appeal that the wording 'without clearly distinguishing their goods from the goods of the plaintiffs should be added'.

Lord Hodson held that the question of law in issue was: was the appellants' description of their goods likely to mislead purchasers into believing that they were the respondents' goods?

> A question of law has arisen that depends on the fact that the appellants, when they use the name Knoll International are honestly using their own name . . . absence of fraud is no defence to an action for passing off, but . . . [the appellants argued] . . . that the honest user of their own name in connection with their goods makes the onus on the plaintiff to satisfy the court that such use by the defendant amounts to a false representation a heavy one.

He rejected the argument, and held that:

> It is inevitable that KNOLL INTERNATIONAL will be shortened to KNOLL . . . the evidence confirmed that if the ordinary person is likely to assume that KNOLL means the respondents he or she would think that KNOLL INTERNATIONAL meant some subsidiary company dealing abroad with the goods of the parent company.

See also the judgments of Lord Guest and Lord Devlin.

It is outside the scope of this book to deal further and in any detail with the questions of confusion which may allegedly arise between similar names (possibly invented or fictitious) under which different businesses are carried on or different goods marketed. However, it is relevant to the subject of personal names (whether original, or borne genuinely for all purposes following a change) to observe that the ordinary prerequisites for a passing off action (*see Erven Warnink Besloten Vennootschap v J Townend & Sons (Hull) Ltd* [1979] AC 731 *below*) apply notwithstanding that the name in question is the plaintiff's own: *Stringfellow v McCain Foods (GB)* (1984) 128 SJ 701.

In the latter case Stringfellow named a nightclub/restaurant 'Stringfellows', which gained widespread publicity and a good reputation. The defendants launched a new frozen chip product called Stringfellows, using dance and music as part of their advertising campaign. In the Court of Appeal the judge referred to the five important elements of passing off cases as laid down by Diplock LJ in the *Erven Warnink* case *below*. He held that Stringfellow was only an ordinary surname, and that there was no misrepresentation by the defendant in the use of the plaintiff's name which could lead persons to believe that there was a business or product association between the plaintiff and the defendant. Although there was an element in the advertising campaign which might lead some to find a connection between the plaintiff and frozen chips, no damage was proved as a result.

In the *Erven Warnink* case (the 'Advocaat case') the five characteristics were set out as follows:

(1) a misrepresentation

(2) made by a trader in the course of trade

(3) to prospective customers of his or ultimate consumers of goods or services supplied by him

(4) which is calculated to injure the business or goodwill of another trader (in the sense that this is a reasonably forseeable consequence) and

(5) which causes actual damage to a business or goodwill of the trader by whom the action is brought, or (in a *quia timet* action) will probably do so.

Moreover, some names which were at first personal have passed into the public domain as having been inveterately applied to some article of a particular kind, or method of production: *see Liebig's Extract of Meat Co v Hanbury* (1867) 17 LT 298, where a claim against the defendants for passing off failed.

In this case a process for making meat extract was discovered in 1847 and 'Liebig's extract of meat' became a well-known term in the scientific world. In 1866 the inventor, Liebig, granted the plaintiff the exclusive right and privilege to use his name in connection with the extract produced by them. The defendants began to sell an Australian extract of meat product manufactured by Tooth after Liebig's process. With the exception of the name there was nothing in common between the packaging of the products.

The plaintiffs sued the defendants to restrain them using the name 'Liebig's extract of meat' and it was held that the term having become a term of art to designate a well-known process long before 1861, the defendants were justified in using it. It was held that the title 'Liebig's extract of meat' was one acquired by the invention (the scientific process) even before the plaintiffs' predecessors ever acquired any interest in it. The process was well recorded and not a secret. The defendants had taken care to distinguish their product as manufactured by Tooth and not the defendants.

Membership of professional associations

The court may grant an injunction to restrain the use of a style, or initials, implying membership of an association. *See Institute of Electrical Engineers v Emerson* (1950) 67 RPC 167 where the defendant used the initials MIEE after his name upon his business notepaper. As he was not a member of the IEE the Institute obtained an injunction to prevent his using the initials. Danckwerts J held that the plaintiffs did not need to carry on a trade. Some connection as to trade is sufficient.

See also Society of Incorporated Accountants v Vincent (1954) 71 RPC 325 where an injunction was granted to restrain the use of the initials FSSA which implied fellowship of the Society, and *R v Piper* [1995] TLR 134, in connection with an offence by Piper under the Trade Descriptions Act 1968, s 14(1)(*a*) by using the logo of the Guild of Master Craftsmen on his notepaper.

Exposure to risk and implication of partnership relationship

An injunction may be granted restraining unauthorised use of another person's name if it might:

(a) expose that other person to a possibility of risk or liability;
(b) amount to a pledge of his credit;
(c) suggest that he is a partner.

It may be an element in a course of deception or be misleading.

In *Routh v Webster* (1847) 10 Beav 561 Routh, who wished to have nothing whatsoever to do with the Economic Conveyance Company whose object was to convey passengers by steamboat and omnibus for 1d per mile, was publicly cited as a trustee of the company in its prospectus, and money was paid into a bank in his name. In the circumstances, the defendants were exposing him to risk which he had not authorised.

It was held that he could not, by the use of his name, be held out as being responsible in connection with the defendants' speculations and potentially involved in liabilities. The defendants could not escape the consequences, saying that their unauthorised inclusion of him in their business operation was the result of mere inadvertence.

In *Burchell v Wilde* [1900] 1 Ch 551 the future use of a solicitors' firm name was not mentioned on dissolution and the matter was left completely undecided. The defendants subsequently used the name Burchell.

Since no one individual's name was used, but only a surname common to the plaintiffs and former, now deceased, partners in the old firm, it was held that the plaintiffs would not be at risk of pecuniary liability. It was important to consider the nature of the business carried on, in order to ascertain whether the plaintiffs' concern was of anticipated annoyance and trouble, or whether there was a substantial pecuniary risk. There was no such risk in this case.

The judge referred to *Levy v Walker above*, where it was pointed out that there was no actual or potential liability for Charbonnel who had changed her name to Levy.

Levy v Walker was examined in *Thynne v Shove* (1890) 45 Ch 577 where it was held that the purchaser of a business and goodwill is not entitled to use the style of the old firm if it includes a living person's name, or its use would expose the person to liability.

The judgment in *Burchell* was confirmed on appeal, where it was further held that in the circumstances each partner could use the name of the old firm subject to the proviso that no one may hold out a former partner, or any other person, as his business partner. That was not the case here.

See also Walter v Ashton [1902] Ch 282 where Byrne J considered the principle to be clear enough, ie the court will not restrain the use of a man's name:

> . . . simply because it is a libel or calculated to cause him injury; but if what is being done is calculated to injure his property, and the probable effect of it will be to expose him to risk or liability then . . . an injunction is the proper remedy.

Byrne J granted an injunction to prevent the defendant from holding out the owners of *The Times* newspaper '. . . either as being principals, or responsibly connected with him, or partners with him in the sale of . . . cycles'. There was a reasonable probability of the owners of *The Times* newspaper having to take steps to disassociate themselves from the defendant in his business advertisements, to avoid being exposed to litigation in connection with the defendant's sale of 'Times' cycles.

Trade relationship

An injunction may also be granted to prevent a person acting in such a way as to imply that he has a trade relationship with the plaintiffs: *see Morris Motors Ltd v Lilley* [1959] 3 All ER 737. Here the plaintiff manufactured cars, which were then sold by authorised dealers or distributors. A sale to L was completed by a dealer. L then sold the car to the defendant, a motor dealer, not authorised by or in a contractual relationship with the plaintiffs. He advertised the car under the new cars' section in a paper as new, for immediate delivery, and sold the car to a purchaser.

The plaintiffs contended the car was not a new car when sold to the purchaser and claimed an injunction to restrain the defendant from advertising, offering for sale or selling any car, not being a new car of the plaintiffs' manufacture, as a new motor car of the plaintiffs' manufacture. It was held that the car was no longer a new car when sold by the authorised dealer, registered with the local authority, supplied with number plates and driven away by the purchaser L.

Since representation that the car was new was likely to damage the plaintiffs, as it amounted to a representation that the defendant was an authorised dealer, an injunction would be granted. Wynn Parry J said it is not necessary to show actual injury, but it is sufficient that that injury might occur, and in this case it might well occur. The defendant represented that he was an authorised dealer selling the car as new and that the plaintiffs had an obligation to service the car.

In *Motor Manufacturers & Traders' Society v Motor Manufacturers' and Traders' Mutual Insurance Co* [1925] Ch 675 the plaintiffs, a well-known motor protection society concerned with the independent promotion and protection of the motor trade and its companies, and known as the SMMT, sued the defendants which had become known as the MMTMI. It was not suggested that the defendant was holding itself out as a member of the plaintiff's company. However, the plaintiffs thought there would be confusion between the two companies and lead to the belief that they were connected in some way.

Lawrence J thought it was possible to account for the choice of the defendant company's name without implication of fraud on the part of its promoters. Its refusal to change its name was consistent with a legitimate claim to the right to retain the name. The only question to be decided therefore was whether as a matter of fact the defendants' name so nearly resembled the plaintiff society's name as to be calculated to deceive.

Lawrence J considered the defendant company's business quite different from and in no way competitive with that of the plaintiff, whose name was descriptive. He considered that where there is no fraud the onus of proving that the adoption of a name exposes the credit or business reputation is heavy. A court must be careful not to grant the plaintiff company a monopoly greater than that to which it is entitled. It was not alleged here that the public would be mistaken or divert their business to the defendants, but rather that there would be a credit or business risk from association or connection if the defendant company were to become insolvent, to dispute its policies of assurance or were otherwise to refuse to honour its obligations.

Domicile of choice

The assumption of a new name, or insistence on a particular way of spelling a name, may be one of a number of factors to be taken into account in considering a person's intention when the question is whether he has acquired a domicile of choice.

In *Drevon v Drevon* (1864) 34 LJ Ch 129, a case involving the domicile of the deceased Charles Henry Drevon, a native of France, it was noted that in his will and upon other occasions when he wrote his name that he spelt it as Henry and not Henri. He also had his son baptised as Henry and not Henri. It was held that this was one reason among many for his having become a domiciled Englishman.

In *Re Martin, Loustalan v Loustalan* [1900] P 211 one element in determining the domicile of Louis Guillard, when he married a French woman named Catherine Euphraise Martin in England, was the fact that he had adopted the English name Martin. He was held domiciled in England, his wife's domicile following his, and her prenuptial will was therefore revoked on marriage.

In *Mary Ann Sells v Arthur Edward Gravenor Rhodes and Walter Empson* (1905) 26 NZLR 87 it was held that the Marquis Arthur James Bertie Taliacarne with an Italian origin of domicile had abandoned that domicile. One factor in this decision was that in the preamble to his will of 1882 he said 'I Arthur James Bertie (heretofore known as Arthur James Bertie Taliacarne) . . .', and signed the will Arthur James Bertie.

He was married in New Zealand as Arthur James Bertie, but gave his father's and mother's names as the Italian Taliacarne and their Italian titles. He then made a further will in 1891 describing himself as 'Arthur James Bertie of Tamahunga Kaipara in the provincial District of Auckland in the Colony of New Zealand gentleman', signing it Arthur James Bertie. It was held established that he had at the time of his death abandoned his Italian domicile and acquired a New Zealand domicile.

Company particulars—directors and secretaries

The Companies Act 1985, s 10 and Sched 1, requires particulars of the first directors and secretary of a company to be delivered to the Registrar, together with the memorandum, in advance of incorporation. The particulars must be in the prescribed form and include, in respect of individuals, the present name and any former names of each director and secretary. 'Name' was substituted by the Companies Act 1989, s 145, Sched 19, para 7(1)-(3) for the former wording in the section 'Christian name and surname'.

The Companies Act 1985, s 305 affects all companies registered in

Great Britain on or after 23 November 1916 under the Companies Acts in force at that time (up to and including the 1985 Act) and all companies, though incorporated outside Great Britain having an established place of business within it.

If a company is subject to s 305 then its correspondence must include the name (formerly the Christian name and surname) of every director on the stationery, unless the name of one or more directors is mentioned only in text or supplied as a signatory. The Christian names or forenames or initials, and surnames of all directors and shadow directors (as defined in the Companies Act 1985, s 741(2)) must be supplied: Companies Act 1985, s 305(4) as substituted by the Companies Act 1989, s 45 and Sched 19, para 4(1),(3).

For the purposes of s 305, 'Christian name' includes a forename, and 'surname' means title, in the case of:

(a) a peer; or

(b) a person with a title other than his surname and by which he is usually known.

Every company must keep a register of directors and secretaries at its registered office: Companies Act 1985, s 288(1).

The particulars of a director (if an individual) must include present and former names. 'Present name', for these purposes, means Christian or other forename and surname. In the case of a peer, or a person normally known by a title, the title may be stated instead of the Christian name or forenames and surname, or in addition to them.

A former name does not include:

(a) the name by which a peer, or a person normally known by a title, was known prior to acquisition of the title;

(b) any former name of a person where that was changed or fell out of use before he attained the age of 18 or which has been changed or out of use for at least 20 years;

(c) the name by which a married woman was known prior to the marriage: Companies Act 1985, s 298(2) as substituted by the Companies Act 1989, s 145, Sched 19, para 2(1),(4).

The particulars of secretaries (including joint secretaries where particulars are to be supplied in respect of each of them) must include present and former names, and the Companies Act 1985, s 298(2) applies to secretaries as to directors, *above.*

Any change in the particulars (including names) contained in the register must be notified in the prescribed form to the Registrar of Companies within 14 days of the change: Companies Act 1985, s 288(2).

Shareholders

The names of every member of a company having a share capital is to be entered on the company's register, which must be altered accordingly when there is any change in the relevant registered details: Companies Act 1985, s 352(2), (3). The courts have power to rectify the register, if necessary, under the Companies Act 1985, s 359.

A change of name by a shareholder may be of concern to company secretaries when registering transfers of shares, or when asked to amend the register in accordance with the change. The primary consideration in such cases is whether the identity of the transferor or applicant is established with the person who previously figured on the register. Subject to the articles, there would be nothing to compel a secretary to insist on any particular form of evidence.

Note the case of *Re Scottish Petroleum* (1883) 23 Ch 413 where Wallace applied for shares in a new company on the understanding from information given in the company prospectus that two certain persons were to be directors of the company. With his allotment letter he received another letter informing him that these two persons had resigned their position. He wrote to the company 12 days later withdrawing his offer to purchase the shares, but the company proceeded to register his name. There was no further communication about the matter. On a winding up of the company it was held that the allotment was not void, in that the letter regarding the resignation did not qualify the letter of allotment preventing it being an unconditional acceptance of Wallace's offer for the shares. However, the allotment was voidable as Wallace's application had been made on the strength of the two persons being directors. He was held liable as a contributory in the winding up because he had not pursued his objection to the allotment in time. He had not done enough to avoid the contract. The time element was important.

See also Re Imperial Chemical Industries Ltd [1936] 2 All ER 463 where it was held that the court could rectify the shareholders' register to replace an original shareholder's name where it had been removed and another's name (Young) entered in respect of the same shares without sufficient cause. The original owner of the shares had been induced to enter a business transaction which involved a transfer of shares, but she alleged she had never signed the required share transfer. In any event, on the facts of the case, the shares registered in Young's name would be held as mere trustee and the original owner was entitled to have them back.

Trade names

The restrictions on trading introduced by the Companies Act 1981, ss 28 and 29, and re-enacted in the Business Names Act 1985, do not appear to involve any particular complication arising from a change of name. A former registration procedure under the Registration of Business Names Act 1916 has been abolished.

The Business Names Act 1985 applies to any person both with a place of business in Great Britain and who carries on business (which term includes profession) there if the business name:

(a) in the case of partnership, inter alia, does not consist of the surnames of all the partners who are individuals;

(b) in the case of an individual, does not consist of his surname without any addition other than one permitted under the Act.

See further the Business Names Act 1985, s 1(1).

Certain additions to the above are are permitted by the Business Names Act 1985, s 1(2):

(a) the forenames (or their initials) of individual partners or, where there are two or more partners with the same surname, the addition of 's' at the end of that surname;

(b) an individual's forename, or its initial;

(c) any addition, in either case, indicating that the business is being carried on in succession to a former owner.

The Act prohibits the use of certain names: *see* Business Names Act 1985, s 2, and certain words and expressions require the approval of the Secretary of State: *see* Business Names Act 1985, s 3.

By virtue of the Business Names Act 1985, s 4 a partnership (or an individual subject to the Act) must supply the name of each partner (or the individual's name) on all business correspondence, written orders for goods or services, invoices and receipts issued and on written demands for payment of debts. A notice containing the names and addresses of the partners (or individuals) must be displayed prominently in any premises where the business is carried on and to which customers have access.

See further the Business Names Act 1985, s 4 as to requirements generally and of companies subject to the Act.

Certain contraventions of the Act's provisions are offences punishable on summary conviction, liability being to a fine: *see* Business Names Act 1985, s 7.

See also the County Court Rules 1981 as applied to business names at p 25 *above*.

Consumer credit

Standard licences granted under the Consumer Credit Act 1974, Pt III for carrying on a consumer credit business or consumer hire business, or under Pt III as applied by s 147(1) to ancillary credit businesses, authorise the licensee to carry on business only under the name or names specified in the licence (s 24). On applying for such a licence a person must satisfy the Director of Fair Trading, inter alia, that the name or names under which he applies is or are not misleading or otherwise undesirable (s 25(1)(*b*)).

A licensee will commit an offence if he holds a standard licence but carries on business under a name which is not mentioned in the licence: Consumer Credit Act 1974, s 39(2). It is possible that a slight variation in the name will not amount to a contravention of the section: *see Peizer v Lefkowitz* [1912] 2 KB 235.

Family members

Generally, it may be thought that a change of surname by a married man living with his wife (or in these more modern times, vice versa) carries a corresponding change in his wife's surname, so long as she does not object. Of course she (or he) always has the right to be known by whatever name she pleases. The surname of any children living with a father or their mother may be similarly affected by way of reputation, but older children particularly may decline to be known by a new name. *See* Chapter 5.

Particular care will need to be taken in the identification of persons in conveyancing and other family matters such as wills and trusts, and any voluntary change of any family member's name should if possible be evidenced by, eg statutory declaration or deed poll, as soon as practicable after a decision to make the change.

Existence of formal evidence will help to clarify exactly those within a family who are affected by a change of name by, eg a husband or wife.

The wording of a name and arms clause may refer to a change of name by 'remoter issue' but this wording would not be acceptable in, eg a statutory declaration or a deed poll. Indeed the Central Office may not enrol a deed which contains this wording, save in exceptional circumstances. A person cannot bind posterity except by attaching an effective condition to the enjoyment of property.

An adult child may adopt the provisions of his parent's deed by endorsing it with a memorandum. *See also* the requirements of the

Enrolment of Deeds (Change of Name) Regulations 1994 (SI No 604) and Chapter 7.

Children whose parents are not married to each other would presumably (subject to what is said *above*) undergo a change of reputed name as a result of a change of the mother's surname. The same consequence might follow on a change of name by a widow, or a woman divorced or separated from her husband, as regards children who remained exclusively with her. *See further* Chapter 5 as to 'parental responsibility' and the Children Act 1989.

In cases of separation or divorce there may be a distinction depending on whether the change is or is not contrived and instantaneous. If the child is of school age before the change, the fact that it will already have been entered by the mother's former name in the school register probably means that a definite step by the mother *vis-à-vis* the school authorities would be necessary in order to effectuate the change. This is what had happened in *Re T (otherwise H) (An Infant)* [1963] Ch 238 and Buckley J, holding that in the absence of special factors it was against the child's interests to deprive it of its father's surname (*see* p 62 *below*), directed the mother to take such steps as were necessary to ensure that the child was called by its proper name as before the purported change. But in *Y v Y (Child: Surname)* [1973] 3 WLR 80 (p 62), Latey J thought the balance was in favour of allowing the change to stand in the case before him, though he deprecated its having been unilaterally initiated. Lane J, in a decision later reversed *(D v B (Surname: Birth Registration)* [1979] Fam 38), went further by directing the mother, until the child reached the age of 18, not to cause *or permit* him to be known by any other surname than that of his father without written consent or court order. The reports of the Court of Appeal decision do not deal with the words italicised, but it is a matter of ordinary experience that mothers might find effective compliance with such an order very difficult.

In these cases there was opposition by the father to the situation created by the attempted change of name which, moreover, coincided approximately with a particular event, namely the mother's remarriage. It is not thought that any of the decisions referred to necessarily precludes the gradual accrual of a young child's reputation in its mother's new name in the absence of protest by the father; though that may be a less likely outcome in a case of remarriage unaccompanied by a change of milieu, for common repute does not readily attribute to a child the surname of its stepfather known to be such. The point of time when the acquisition of the new name was complete would be determined as a question of fact (*see* Chapter 2) and thereafter, it is conceived, the name might be used with impunity. Indeed it would be said to be wrong to use any other.

The legal position cannot, however, be regarded as firmly established, and where it is possible to execute a deed poll on the child's behalf, and to enrol it with the father's consent (or by leave in circumstances which justify dispensing with that consent), it seems better to do so to ensure an effective change of the child's name. *See* Chapters 5 and 7 and in particular the Enrolment of Deeds (Change of Name) Regulations 1994 (SI No 604), reg 8 and *Practice Direction (Child: Change of Surname)* [1995] 1 FLR 458.

Criminal matters

The general freedom to change one's name may, again, provide no answer to a criminal charge if the change amounts to deception and a pecuniary advantage is obtained, contrary to the Theft Act 1968 or some other provision of the criminal law.

In Scotland it has been held to be a relevant averment that A falsely stated that his name was B in order to obtain a certificate of motor insurance: *Clark v Chalmers* 1961 SLT 325. *See* pp 5–6 for the facts of this case.

Mistake

A change of name, though in itself perfectly legitimate, may occasion a mistake on the part of a person intending to make a contract as to the identity of the person with whom he is contracting. As to the circumstances in which such a mistake might nullify or negative consent to the purported agreement, *see Halsbury's Laws of England* 4th edn (Butterworth & Co), vol 9, paras 290–293.

Other instances

In *Watson v Lucas* (1980) 124 SJ 513 little weight was given by the Court of Appeal to the retention by persons cohabiting of their own names, when the question was whether he was a member of her family for Rent Act purposes.

A man and a woman had cohabited for 19 years, she being the protected tenant of the property of which the plaintiff sought possession on her death. He, claiming a statutory succession, was denied the same by the judge at first instance on the basis that each had kept their own name throughout cohabitation. On appeal this was held to be an error of law. He should not be denied Rent Act protection on the basis that he had chosen not to obtain a divorce and that he and the protected tenant had each kept their own names.

There may be various official records or documents to be adjusted in consequence of a change of name. *See*, eg as to driving licences, the Road Traffic Act 1988, s 99(4), (5), (7), (8) and regulations thereunder, and s 168 as to the failure to give a name or the giving of a false name in a case or reckless, careless or inconsiderate driving or cycling.

Self-regulating associations

Self-regulating associations will have their own rules providing for procedure on a change of name of its members. For example, *The Financial Intermediaries Managers and Brokers Regulatory Association (FIMBRA) Rules* (FIMBRA, 1991) (which came into effect on 1 January 1992) deals with the matter under 'Changes: You and Your Business', which is addressed to all members and their registered individuals. *See* particularly r 11.3 and 11.4.

Chapter 4

Name Clauses in Wills and Settlements

Name and arms clauses generally

A will or settlement may contain a name and arms clause for the purpose of obliging one or more beneficiaries to take the testator's or settlor's name (and possibly also bear his arms) as a condition of his entitlement to the interest in the property. This chapter concentrates on the name element in these clauses, although many of the cases referred to contain the arms element.

A well-drafted name clause will clearly set out the names or classes of individuals who must comply with the obligation, if they do not already bear and use the specified name, and state the period and the manner of compliance.

Complementing the name clause, there is usually a defeasance clause (otherwise known as a forfeiture or shifting clause) defeating the interest of a person not complying with the obligation, in favour of the next person to take under the settlement.

The validity of name and defeasance clauses, which have been used as far back as 1787, will depend on the drafting: *see generally Re Neeld, Carpenter v Inigo-Jones* [1962] Ch 643. The less precise the wording, the greater the chance of the clause being considered void:

    (a) for impossibility;

    (b) for uncertainty;

    (c) as against the rule against perpetuities;

    (d) as against public policy,

or perhaps construed in a manner different to that which a settlor may have actually intended. *See Re Lewis's Will Trusts, Whitelaw v Beaumont* [1951] 2 TLR 1032 where the wording of the clause that the beneficiary had to assume a surname 'S . . .' so that 'it be the last or principal surname' was held void for uncertainty.

A name and arms clause which in substance follows the language in the precedent books cannot be challenged as being too vague and un- certain. Therefore an obligation to take a surname and use it on all ordinary occasions is sufficiently clear and precise, as is a divesting provision expressed to take effect if a donee should at any time disuse or discontinue to use the adopted surname: *see ibid* at pp 667 and 679 (Lord Evershed MR). For forms see Prideaux, *Conveyancing Precedents* 25th edn, vol 3, pp 281–284 and 797–800, and the *Encyclopaedia of Forms and Precedents* 5th edn (Butterworth & Co) vol 40, p 728–9, form 407.

A court may not be able to remodel a clause so as to make it sensible and effective (*see Re Neeld above* at pp 671 and 672). To do so may involve a complete departure from what the testator said. Upjohn J said it is the duty of the court to apply the ordinary canons of construction to make sense of the language. In *Re Neeld (see above)* there were two name and arms clauses, the terms of which are set out *below*. The case dealt with several facets of the law relating to name and arms clauses and it is appropriate to set out the two will clauses here for reference.

The first which applied to specific devises required:

> . . . any person who . . . shall . . . become entitled to the actual receipt of the yearly rents and profits of [the properties] and who shall not then use the surname of Inigo-Jones or if an infant shall so become entitled then within the space of one year next after he or she shall have attained the age of twenty-one years take upon himself and use upon all occasions the surname of Inigo-Jones only . . . and shall within the space of one year next after the period hereinbefore prescribed apply for and endeavour to obtain a proper licence from the Crown or take such other means as may be requisite to enable him or her to take use and bear the surname of Inigo-Jones only . . . and in case any of the said persons . . . shall refuse or neglect or discontinue to take or use such surname and arms and to take such means as may be requisite for the purpose of taking or using the same then after the expiration of the said space of one year the use and estate hereby limited . . . shall absolutely cease and [the properties] . . . shall [devolve as though] . . . the person were then actually dead.

The second clause which applied to the residuary estate stated that:

> . . . every person who . . . shall become entitled to the actual receipt of the yearly rents and profits of [the property] and who shall not then use the surname of 'Neeld' and bear the arms of 'Neeld' . . . shall within the space of one year next after he or she shall so become entitled as aforesaid or if an infant shall so become entitled then within the space of one year next after he or she shall have attained the age of 21 years take upon himself or herself and use upon all occasions the surname of 'Neeld' only . . . and shall within the space of one year next after the periods hereinbefore prescribed

apply for and endeavour to obtain an Act of Parliament or a proper licence from the Crown . . . and to take such means as may be requisite for the purpose of taking and using the same then after the expiration of the said space of one year the use and estate hereby limited to the person who or whose husband shall so refuse neglect or discontinue as aforesaid . . . shall absolutely cease . . .

Before any assents had been made or the net residue ascertained, the executor took out a summons to determine, inter alia, whether the clauses were valid and binding on the testator's grandson and brother respectively. *See further below.*

Void for impossibility

A name clause may be altogether void for impossibility: *see Re Parrott, Cox v Parrott* [1946] Ch 183, where Vaisey J stated that:

Where the legatee is of a different Christian name from the testator he cannot of course part with his own Christian name nor can he take that of the testator except as part of a compound surname consisting of the Christian and surname of the testator.

He could also take the specified Christian name as an additional forename, but it would in all events be a question of construction of the particular clause whether this course constituted compliance.

Compliance with wording of clause

The precise wording of the clause will be important for a court in determining whether or not it has been complied with, and whether or not it is void, eg for uncertainty or impossibility.

'Alone or together with'

A phrase such as 'alone or together with' can be construed as giving the beneficiary the choice of using the required name before or after the existing name: *see Re Eversley, Mildmay v Mildmay* [1900] 1 Ch 96.

In this case it was held that the use of the prescribed name before the devisee's own name was sufficient to comply with the clause in the will. Byrne J held that the clause had obviously been taken from a regular precedent, and was of the opinion that the clause did not require the applicant (St John Mildmay) to take and use the name of Shaw-Lefevre after the family surname. The words 'alone or together with' were the key words.

The case of *D'Eyncourt v Gregory* (1876) 1 Ch D 441 was distinguished in that there the appropriate words were 'assume and take upon himself . . . and use. . . the surname of Gregory'. Putting Gregory before the name Welby was not sufficient compliance. Here there was no choice for the beneficiary; Gregory alone was to be the new surname.

'Assume'

In *Re Llangattock, Shelley v Harding* (1917) 33 TLR 250 the will of the late Lord Shelley contained a provision that everyone who became entitled in possession to the settled estate should assume the surname and arms of Rolls, there being a defeasance clause in the event of non-compliance. Lady Shelley applied to the court to determine whether she would comply with the condition if she took the name of Rolls in one of the following alternatives:

(a) taking the surname Rolls before Shelley with a hyphen in between;
(b) as in (a) but without a hyphen;
(c) taking the surname Rolls after Shelley with a hyphen in between;
(d) as in (c) but without a hyphen.

It was held that options (a) and (b) would not comply, but either (c) or (d) would.

'Take and use'

In *Re Berens* [1926] Ch 596 it was held that, although special words in the clause may authorise the particular position or choice of positions of a name, a requirement to 'take and use' a particular surname was not satisfied by placing the new name in front of the existing surname. The composite name of Berens-Dowdeswell did not satisfy the requirement.

Upon all occasions

If a beneficiary is to 'take and use' a particular surname within a specified time after becoming entitled, a continued use of the surname after that specified time is to be implied: *see Re Drax, Dunsany (Baroness) v Sawbridge* [1906] 75 LJ Ch 317 where there was a defeasance clause if the beneficiary should 'refuse or neglect to take or use such surname as aforesaid and in manner aforesaid'.

Here the will required the use of the surnames Erle and Drax either alone or in addition to and after the original surname in deeds and documents, and on all other occasions. The beneficiary had a time limit within which to apply for and endeavour to obtain a Royal Licence, or take other steps to enable her to use the name as required. If the beneficiary refused or neglected, the forfeiture condition operated.

The plaintiff obtained a Royal Licence to take and use and bear the name and arms of Erle and Drax in addition to her existing names of Plunkett and Ernle, and she did so within the time limit.

In social matters and in letters and the ordinary business of life she used 'Ernle Lady Dunsany' and applied to the court for a ruling that except for the purposes of deeds or formal documents describing her, she should not usually in correspondence or socially be described by any name other than her title.

Swinfen Eady J held that, in his opinion, 'upon all other occasions' meant when it was right to use a surname and those occasions when a surname is ordinarily used, but it did not apply to occasions where surnames are not commonly used. The obligation would include affidavits and extend to writings of a formal character, but would not mean every letter or extend to visiting cards.

This case was applied in *Re Howard's Will Trusts* [1961] 2 All ER 413 where the appropriate words were ' . . . in all deeds and writings which he or she shall sign and upon all occasions . . .' It was held that 'on all occasions' referred to all occasions on which a surname was used, and not to Christian name occasions or nickname occasions.

In *Re Neeld, Carpenter v Inigo-Jones* [1962] Ch 643 at p 682, Lord Upjohn said that he could not see how there could be:

> . . . any uncertainty in a direction to a beneficiary that if he wishes to enter into the ocupation of valuable settled estates, he must bear a name and arms or assume and use on all ordinary occasions a name and arms other than his own.

Changing one's name can take some time, but after that 'a person who was formerly ordinarily called X becomes ordinarily known as Y'. Although the new name might have to be used on all occasions there would of course be some mistakes resulting from forgetfulness, and even after a year Lord Upjohn thought this should be treated as *de minimis*.

Lord Diplock held that there was no uncertainty when it came to the meaning of a clause drafted '. . . to take upon himself and use upon all occasions . . .', and an occasional inadvertent use of the former name would not amount to a discontinuance.

Time for compliance

If there is no time limit for compliance with the condition then, taking into account the circumstances of the case, a reasonable time will suffice:

see Davies v Lowndes (1835) 1 Bing NC 597 at p 618. Of course, there may be circumstances where the clause is void for infringing the rule against perpetuities: *see Re Fry, Reynolds v Denne* [1945] Ch 348. In this case there was no defeasance clause providing for shifting the estate in the event of non-compliance with the name clause, which was expressed to be a condition appurtenant to the taking of the gift, but held to be a condition subsequent and void.

In *Re Neeld* the question arose regarding Clause 14 as to whether the prescribed periods began with the death of the testator, or the later date of an assent; and regarding Clause 17 as to what was the period within which the provisions were to be complied with.

Cross J in the lower court ([1960] Ch 455) held that as regards Clause 14 (re the composite gift of residuary realty and personalty), the beneficiary had not become entitled to the income of the net residuary estate since it had not yet been ascertained, and the one-year period within which he had to take the name and arms of Neeld had not begun to run against him. This was not appealed.

As regards Clause 17 (re the specifically devised realty), he held that the beneficiary had a vested interest in the yearly rents and profits of such realty as from the testator's death and had, accordingly, become 'entitled to the actual receipt of the yearly rents' within Clause 17 on the testator's death. Since more than a year had elapsed since the death of the testator the beneficiary had forfeited his interest. This was appealed.

The Court of Appeal held that the beneficiary:

> had not become entitled to the 'actual receipt' of the specifically devised properties and that, as a result of the property legislation of 1925, he would not become entitled to the 'actual receipt' of such rents and profits until the date on which the legal estate in the devised properties was vested in him by a vesting assent or conveyance, or he became entitled to require the personal representatives to execute such a vesting assent or conveyance.

That point in the administration not having been arrived at, 'he had not yet to decide whether he would assume the name and arms of Inigo-Jones'.

Diplock LJ, confirming the opinion of Cross J, held that there was a time limit of one year for compliance with the provisions. But when did the year commence? Cross J had held this to be the date of the testator's death. On construction of the relevant law relating to the administration of estates, Diplock J held that there was no doubt that the personal representatives became accountable to the life tenant for the yearly rents and profits of the specifically devised land received by them from the date of the testator's death. At p 688, he said:

I do not think that the life tenant can properly be said to be himself entitled to the 'actual receipts' of such yearly rents and profits until the date on which either the legal estate becomes vested in him, by a vesting assent or conveyance executed by the personal representatives or he becomes entitled to require the personal representatives to pay over the yearly rents and profits to him. [Such a date] coincides with that on which he is entitled to require the personal representatives to execute a vesting assent. This deferment of his entitlement . . . arises from the operation of the relevant legislation upon the trusts of the will itself.

No vesting assent having yet been executed, the question then arose as to whether the beneficiary was entitled to call for one to be executed. He was not: there were matters which might provide justification for the executors refusing to execute a vesting assent. Upjohn LJ said:

It is reasonable that, if the beneficiary is to choose whether to change his name or forfeit his interest in the property, he must know exactly what the property is, and the estate duty charges, and he can only know this for certain when the administration has reached a stage where he is entitled to require the executors to execute a conveyance to him of the property specifically devised.

Until the estate was cleared, it could not be said that the devisee was in actual receipt of the rents and profits of the property.

Construction of defeasance clauses

The validity of conditions imposed by will or settlement on the entitlement of an individual to take a benefit thereunder may vary according to whether the requirement is, on its proper construction:
  (a) a condition precedent;
  (b) a condition subsequent; or
  (c) a defeasance clause.
Regarding the latter, *see Re Tepper's Will Trusts, Kramer v Ruda* [1987] Ch 358, a case involving conditions as to beneficiaries remaining within the Jewish faith and not marrying outside it.

Defeasance clauses (alternatively known as shifting or forfeiture clauses) are inserted in wills and settlements to shift an interest in an estate from a beneficiary on the happening of a specified contingent event. They are often used to impose a penalty for failure to comply with a condition in a settlement, eg a name and arms clause.

Lord Evershed in *Re Neeld above,* at p 667, held that a defeasance clause must be drawn with such a degree of certitude that the court:

. . . upon a fair construction of the language used according to its ordinary sense [is able to] arrive at a clear conclusion what truly is the obligation which the donor intends to impose, and what are the event or events which he has in mind as causing a divesting of the estate.

An example of a defeasance clause which operated is in *Barlow v Bateman* (1735) 2 Bro Parl Cas 271. Barlow left a legacy of £1,000 to his daughter provided that she should marry a man who bore the name and arms of Barlow, with a substituted gift to the plaintiff should she not do so. The daughter married a man called Bateman who assumed the name Barlow only about three weeks prior to the marriage.

Although the lower court held that the condition was complied with, the House of Lords on appeal reversed the decision on the basis that anyone could take what surname and as many surnames as he wished and without having to obtain an Act of Parliament.

A condition subsequent, divesting the estate if a beneficiary should 'refuse or neglect' to take a new name and arms, had been held not to apply so as to deprive a minor. This was because the words contemplate a degree of volition of which a young child is incapable, and it is not possible (for the purposes of construction of a will) to draw a line at any particular age short of majority when it could be said that it is possible for an infant to 'refuse or neglect' to take the new name: *Re Edwards, Lloyd v Boyes* [1910] 1 Ch 541. For the facts of this case *see* p 61.

Post-war restrictive construction

There were several post-war cases in which name clauses were restrictively construed (a tendency halted apparently in the Court of Appeal in *Re Neeld above*).

In *Re Lewis's Will Trusts* [1951] 2 TLR 1032 Vaisey J held that the word 'disuse' involved a continuous process, the beginning of which was very difficult to establish. He distinguished 'discontinuance' as an overt act that might be too uncertain for effectiveness, but he expressed no final view on this point. On the construction of the particular clause in question it was held void for uncertainty.

Subsequently in *Re Bouverie, Bouverie v Marshall* [1952] Ch 400 the testator settled his estate on condition that any life tenant (or in the case of a married woman, her husband) should assume the name Bouverie either with or without his own proper surname within one year of becoming entitled in possession. However, if he or she 'at any time afterwards disuse such surname . . .' stated gifts over would take effect.

Vaisey J, following *Re Lewis above*, held that the condition was a condition subsequent, but doubted if it could be of effect as it was not 'of sufficient high degree of certitude and precision which is required'. The fact that the word 'disuse' might be plain in the colloquial sense was not enough. It had to be seen from the beginning precisely and distinctly on what event Mrs Marshall's life interest were to determine. If she stopped using the name once and for all, that was clear, but the question lay open over other instances. The clause was vague and uncertain.

In *Re Wood's Will Trusts, Wood v Donnelly* [1952] Ch 406 Wynn Parry J followed *Re Bouverie* and held that 'discontinue to bear and use' was no different in meaning from 'disuse'. There was no valid distinction between the two. He followed Vaisey J in holding the clause void for uncertainty.

He held that the proper approach is not what a party must ask himself, or what difficulties a party faces on reading the will, but whether a court can attribute a sufficiently precise meaning to the clause.

In *Re Kersey, Alington v Alington* [1952] WN 541 the plaintiff, a married woman, became tenant for life. The long name clause tried to cover every eventuality, the wording in question being 'refuse or neglect . . . or if any person already having borne and used . . . should discontinue to use and bear'. Danckwerts J held it failed for uncertainty.

In the light of *Re Neeld above*, *Re Bouverie*, *Re Woods* and *Re Kersey* are clearly no longer reliable. However, the wording in these cases was less explicit than in *Re Neeld*, and in that case Cross J had succeeded in distinguishing them ([1960] Ch 455).

Vaisey J in *Re Parrott above* seems to have thought that if the requirement was simply 'to assume' the new name, and did not state the duration or occasions of user, that it then might be void for uncertainty. However, the tenor of the judgment in *Re Neeld* is not to support any such distinction. One precedent quoted with apparent approval merely says 'shall assume' the name and divests the estate if the beneficiary should 'disuse it'.

In *Re Howard's Will Trusts, Levin v Bradley* [1961] 2 All ER 413 the testator settled three estates, subject to a name clause, that every person becoming entitled should within one year 'take and use and bear' or, if already using the name, 'continue to bear' the particular name 'on all occasions, and if they should refuse or neglect to take the new name, or if using it, should discontinue to use it then their estate should determine'.

No steps had been taken by anyone concerned in the three settlements, and it was held on the question of validity of the clause that in this case it *was* expressed with sufficient precision and certainty to enable the court and the parties to see from the beginning exactly what had to be done to avoid or bring about a determination of the relevant interest. Wilberforce J held that the clause had clearly been drafted by a person with a sound knowledge of the precedents and case law.

The word 'discontinue' was clear and certain in its context and meant that one case of failure led to forfeiture. Even one instance would be a breach. The will did not refer to a fixed period of cessation—the name had to be used 'on all occasions'.

See also Re Drax, Dunsany (Baroness) v Sawbridge (1906) 75 LJ Ch 317 which was applied in *Re Howard's Will Trusts above*, where it was held that if a time is limited for the act of assumption, discontinuance at any time before or after the expiry of the limit will lead to forfeiture.

It is, however, important to be clear in drafting. In *Re Murray, Martins Bank v Dill* [1955] Ch 69 the Court of Appeal declined to uphold either of two clauses, one of which was confusedly expressed and in apparent conflict with the other.

Clause 8 of the testator's will stated that:

> Every person . . . shall assume the surname of Murray either alone or in substitution of his or her usual surname (yet so that the name of Murray shall be the last or usual name).

Clause 9 contained certain divesting provisions if the beneficiary refused or neglected to assume the surname of Murray within one year after becoming entitled in possession, and Clause 10 contained the testator's earnest wish and desire that every person who became tenant for life of the Coles Park estate (or in the case of a married woman, her husband) should continue to use the surname of Murray so long as they were entitled to possession of the estate.

It was held that the court could not see from the beginning precisely and distinctly on the happening of what event the preceding vested estate was to determine. There were three doubts about the clauses. The first was as to the word 'assume' in Clause 8. When read with Clause 10, the obligation to continue to use was negated. Normally 'assume' would involve at least some degree of use, and without Clause 10 it might have been thought that 'assume' meant 'take and use'.

The second doubt revolved round the words '. . . either alone or in substitution . . .' Evershed MR thought that if there had been a mere slip, then he could have put it right, but it was not absolutely clear here that there was a slip, and if so what it was. He would not read into the clause 'words that would assist a forfeiture'. The absence of precision lead to a real doubt as to what extent Murray was to be made part of a surname.

The third doubt went to the meaning of the arms part of the clause. The name and arms part of the codicil was declared void, but on the very special provisions in the clause which were thought too uncertain to permit of the validity of the clause. Evershed MR said in this case that he was not expressing any opinion on the validity of the recent decisions as set out above.

In *Re Neeld above* [1962] Ch 643 the testator had used the words:

> . . . and in case any of the said persons shall refuse or neglect or discontinue to take or use such surname and arms

or to take the required steps

> after the expiration of the said space of one year the use and estate hereby limited to the person who or whose husband shall so refuse neglect or discontinue as aforesaid shall . . . absolutely cease.

Lord Evershed MR said he thought there was no real ambiguity in a divesting provision expressed to take effect if a person should at any time 'disuse or discontinue to use' the surname which they had adopted, though there might be circumstances where a disuse from accident or in some other special circumstances would seriously raise the question of its application.

Upjohn LJ thought the words at first sight gave rise to some difficulty:

> I think the words 'refuse, neglect or discontinue' must be read distributively, that is to say, there is a forfeiture on the happening of either of two events: (1) in the case of a person who refuses or neglects within the space of one year to take the name and bear the arms, or (2) if having taken the name and arms he thereafter at any time discontinues the use of the name or bearing of the arms. This construction seems to me a reasonable one.

He saw no uncertainty in a defeasance if the beneficiary disused or discontinued to use a name and he saw no difference between these verbs for this purpose.

Failure to invest a gift over

A name clause may be ineffective unless there is a gift over in the event of a beneficiary failing to comply with it.

In *Gulliver d Corrie v Ashby* (1766) 4 Burr 1929 one of the provisions of William Wykes's will was that:

> . . . provided always that this devise is expressly upon the condition that whenever it shall happen . . . that the person or persons to whom the [mansion house and estates] from time to time shall descend or come . . . shall then change their surname and take upon them and their heirs the surname of Wykes only and not otherwise.

There was no devise over on default. The defendant's predecessor in possession had never changed his name, and Lord Aston held that the 'condition' 'only operated as a recommendation or desire . . . the testator had not intended that the estate should cease on non-performance of the condition'. It was not intended to be compulsory.

The case was applied in *Re Evans's Contract* [1920] 2 Ch 469 where there was no gift over on non-compliance with the proviso in the testator's will. It was held that where a beneficiary (Mrs Evans) failed to take the specified name (Storer) within 12 months of becoming entitled in possession, in accordance with the provision in the will, she could still make good title on a sale of her interest.

The court did not consider that the clause caused the estate to go over on non-compliance, as if Mrs Evans were dead. It was, rather, a declaration of the testator's desire.

See also *Re Talbot* [1932] IR 714 where it was held that the particular obligation on the beneficiary was a mere request or expression of the testator's desire without any coercive legal effect. *See* Chapter 5, p 61 for the facts of this case.

In *Re Fry, Reynolds v Denne* [1945] Ch 348 there was a 'condition appurtenant' that the beneficiary must 'take and continue to bear my surname'. The beneficiary applied to the court to determine:

(a) when she had to take the testator's name;
(b) over what period she had to bear it; and
(c) whether she could put it in front of and together with her own surname.

It was held that the clause was a condition subsequent and void. There was no gift over on a breach of the condition, despite the fact the testator was quite clear as to his wishes. It was also contrary to public policy (*see further below*), forcing the use of a testator's surname on the beneficiary both while she was unmarried and married.

Public policy

The other objection to name and arms clauses much canvassed in post-war years was on the ground of public policy.

This objection was partially accepted by the courts of first instance, which held clauses to be void in so far as they placed on a married woman an obligation to take a surname other than her husband's. *See Re Fry above*, where Vaisey J took the view that the clause requiring the testator's eldest daughter to take and continue to bear his surname was void as contrary to public policy.

He considered this type of condition to be irksome, but no more than when applied to a man, and there could be some circumstances when it could be applied to a woman, eg if she were the sole surviving member of an important family. In this case there were no such circumstances.

The clause required the woman to use the name both during spinsterhood and her marriage 'possibly to a succession of men with a number of different surnames'. The use of the name would lead to embarrassment and inconvenience for children, for relatives and socially. Unlike a pen or theatre name the use was required to be continuous. Even though in this case the husband was prepared to change his own name 'not every husband would be equally accommodating or sensible'.

In the next reported case on the matter, *Re Lewis's Will Trusts* [1951] 2 TLR 1032, Vaisey J felt unable to distinguish this case and so followed *Re Fry*, holding that the clause which affected an unmarried woman was again against public policy.

In *Re Howard's Will Trusts, Levin v Bradley* [1961] Ch 507 Wilberforce J held that the clause was void in the case of a married woman, but valid in the case of men and widows.

He cited *Re Kersey, Alington v Alington* [1952] WN 541 (where the *ratio decidendi* of the case applied to married women only) in which it was held to be against public policy that a married woman should be put in the position of putting pressure on her husband so that she might keep her estate. 'It illustrated the fatuity of trying to impose obligations . . . which were out of date and inconsistent with the spirit of the times.' It was not desirable that a husband be put under pressure by his wife to change his name in order that she could take her interest in an estate. This was calculated to cause differences between them. *See also Re Harris's Will Trusts* (1961) *The Times*, 1 March, following *Re Kersey*.

In *Re Delmé-Radcliffe* (1961) 105 SJ 529 the plaintiff was to marry a man who was unwilling to change his name to the required Delmé-Radcliffe either before or after the marriage. Buckley J held he was bound, as had Wilberforce J in *Re Howard's Will Trusts above*, to follow the series of decisions where name and arms clauses were held to be against public policy in so far as they applied to married women.

He could not find grounds to distinguish *Re Fry above*, where the condition was imposed upon married women without including their husbands, and so he followed it. He expressed the opinion that there was no reason that, because it was against public policy to enforce a condition against a particular class, that the condition could not be effective as against beneficiaries who were not members of the class.

The will provided that the clause applied to *every* person who became entitled as tenant-in-tail in possession to the property. Here the clause was not binding on the plaintiff while she was an infant or thereafter while her father was alive, or at any time while she was a married woman.

All these cases must now, however, be read in the light of *Re Neeld* [1962] Ch 643. In this case Lord Evershed MR said that even though many might consider this type of clause 'silly', it was for Parliament rather than the courts to decide if clauses of this kind, which had been part of the conveyancing system for very many years, were to be treated as contrary to public policy.

Diplock LJ could not persuade himself that the marriage bond was:

> so frail as to be in danger of falling asunder in the agony of a joint decision by husband and wife as to whether the latter should accept a benefaction at the cost of either or both changing their surname.

There, short of the House of Lords, the matter rests. In another context (defeasance if the tenant in possession should be a Roman Catholic) the House firmly upheld the freedom of testamentary disposition as part of public policy: *see Blathwayt v Cawley (Baron)* [1976] AC 397, a case showing remarkable judicial differences on the construction of the relevant clause in a will.

The right form of a name clause, where the beneficiary is or may become a married woman, is to place the obligation on the husband as well; for although there is nothing in law to compel a married woman to use her husband's surname, the consequences of a clause which in effect requires her not to do so are embarrassing and inconvenient: *see Re Lewis' Will Trusts* [1951] 2 TLR 1032.

Chapter 5

Children's Names

Introduction

It can be stated as a general principle that in the United Kingdom parents have always had the right to choose and change their children's names. A child will normally acquire both his first name, or Christian name, and his surname from his parents. In a family where the parents are married the child will normally, but not necessarily, bear the surname of the father, or it may be registered with the mother's name. Where the parents are not married the child might bear its mother's or its father's name, depending on, eg whether the parents live together. *See further* as to registration of birth, Chapter 6.

A parent might formally evidence a change of a child's name for a specific purpose, eg to satisfy a condition in a will or a settlement, or as part of a voluntary deed, or perhaps for some other reason personal to the family. A parent may alternatively allow a child to acquire a new name informally by use and reputation. *See below* and Chapter 2. An example of a 'formal' change is where a Royal Licence for the assumption of an additional surname by the infant grandson of the grantee was recorded in the *London Gazette* on 28 October 1960.

There are two statutory restrictions on changing a child's name. *See below* at pp 71–3.

Change by use and reputation

Whether or not there has been a change of name by use and reputation will be a question of fact in each case. A change of name by a parent, particularly the one with whom the child lives and depends upon, whether on remarriage or otherwise, and especially if accompanied by a change in residence, may lead either immediately or in the course of time to a 'passive' change in the child's surname.

A very young child may undergo a change of name by use and reputation without any conscious decision on his part, or indeed on the part of anyone else. See *Doe d Luscombe v Yates* (1822) 5 B & Ald 544.

In *James v McLennan* 1971 SLT 162, HL, a case regarding entitlement to an estate, Henrietta Howatson (an unmarried mother) changed her son's surname to McInnes when she married the (presumed) father of the boy three years after his birth. The child never had any suspicion that he had ever been anything but his father's lawful son which, it was held, could not have happened unless his name had been changed (probably before he went to school) before he was of sufficient age to be aware of the situation.

In *Dancer v Dancer* [1949] P 147 Ormrod J held that a surname used exclusively by and of a person from the time she was three years old, when her mother went to live with another man, until she was 20 years' old, had effectively been substituted for her original surname.

However, an older child of 16 or more, in today's modern and sophisticated lifestyle, will usually be called by the name he chooses to use and be known by. He might be expected to be able, by protest or action, to curtail or prevent the growth of an unsought reputation, or at all events not to acquiesce by himself in the use of a name of which he disapproves; or alternatively to use and encourage the use of a new name to be substituted in time for his original name. There is an element of volition.

However, there have been doubts concerning the effectiveness of a change of name when initiated by voluntary action on the part of a child. In *Re Edwards, Lloyd v Boyes* [1910] 1 Ch 541 there was a condition subsequent in a will divesting the estate if a beneficiary should 'refuse or neglect' to assume the name and arms of Edwards within six months after he became entitled in possession. It was held that, in this case, a child (ie a minor) could not be deprived of the estate, because 'refusing or neglecting' involved exercising discretion and volition, which as an infant in law he had no power to do. This applied whatever age the child might be. It was stated obiter, however, that an infant of five, if the matter were explained to him, might choose to be called by a certain name.

In *Re Talbot* [1932] IR 714 a child of 12 was entitled to a life interest in an estate provided he assumed the testator's surname as his last and principal name. It was held that: 'It is impossible for an infant to accomplish the act of taking or assuming a surname by any voluntary action on his part'. This would involve the exercise of discretion and will of which the child was not legally competent, and there is a very important difference between the acquisition of a name by a child by repute and his actually voluntarily taking or assuming a new name.

In *Re T (otherwise H) (An Infant)* [1963] Ch 238 Buckley J, in dealing with a case where a deed poll had been executed on behalf of a nine-year-old girl, said:

> ... a change of name on the part of an adult must, in my judgment, involve a conscious decision on the part of the adult that he wishes to change his name and be generally known by his new name. An infant, and certainly not an infant of the age of the infant with whom I am concerned in the present case, is not competent to make such a decision.

Today, the older child's conscious decision making power is recognised in the Enrolment of Deeds (Change of Name) Regulations 1994 (SI No 604), reg 8(3). This states that if the child has attained 16 years a deed poll evidencing a change of his name must have the child's consent endorsed upon it by signature of the child both in his old and new names. *See further* Chapter 7.

Disagreements as to changing a child's name

This usually happens where there is a separation of the parents. In particular where there is a divorce, the courts treat the question as one of real importance as affecting the interests and welfare of the child. *See W v A (Child: Surname)* [1981] 1 All ER 100, as compared with the earlier cases where the question was thought to occupy too much attention in disputes over children.

Position prior to commencement of the Children Act 1989

Prior to 14 October 1991 an order or agreement giving either or both parents custody of their child did not confer on that spouse the sole control of the child's surname.

The true position was stated by Latey J in *Y v Y* [1973] Fam 147 where he referred to the views expressed by Buckley J in *Re T above*. Both were cases in which the court had awarded custody of children to the mothers. The fathers had access (by order or in fact). The mothers had remarried and sought, without the fathers' consent, to confer upon the children their own new married names.

Latey J came to the conclusion that after a custody order, neither party could unilaterally cause a child's name to be changed. The father and mother each had rights which must not be infringed by the other.

The above and similar decisions were perpetuated in a rule of court by which (unless otherwise directed) any order of a divorce court which gave a parent custody or care and control of a child had to provide that no step (other than the institution of proceedings in any court) might be taken by that parent which would result in the child being known by a new surname before he or she attained the age of 18 (or being female, married under that age), except with the leave of a judge or the consent in writing of the other parent. *See* (the now lapsed) Matrimonial Causes Rules 1977 (SI No 344), r 92(8). These Rules have been replaced by the Family Proceedings Rules 1991 (as amended).

On the face of it, this rule prohibited more than just a unilateral change by deed poll: the parent was inhibited from taking any step in the direction of a change in the child's surname. Such a step might consist, eg of the use of a new name when entering the child at a school. Yet if the child were below school age it might become known by a new name, eg the name of the mother on remarriage, without the custodial parent taking any action at all, and perhaps without her being able to prevent it. To this extent it could perhaps be respectfully doubted whether this rule, or an order made in its terms, could be said to be fully effective in all cases. Ormrod J said in *R(BM) v R(DN) (Child: Surname)* [1977] 1 WLR 1256 that the rule was directed only to formal changes. It did not in any case apply according to its context where a custody order was made in a case before the magistrates. There the Matrimonial Causes Rules 1977 had no application.

Position as from commencement of the Children Act 1989

The Children Act 1989 ('CA 1989'), which was brought into force (mainly) on 14 October 1991, introduced a new concept applicable to all parents as from that date—that of 'parental responsibility'. This potentially gives a range of persons the right and power to change a child's name.

However, a person will not be able to act inconsistently with the terms of a court order existing as at 14 October 1991, and such orders will continue until varied, discharged or expired. Where a residence order is made an existing order is immediately discharged. *See* CA 1989, s 108, Sched 14 for transitional provisions. Existing rights will be protected while the new concept applies.

Definitions
The following definitions in the CA 1989 may assist the reader throughout the remainder of this chapter.

(1) 'Care order'—(subject to CA 1989, s 105(1)) an order placing a child with respect to whom an application is made in the care of a designated local authority, and includes an interim care order made under CA 1989, s 38: CA 1989, s 31(11).

(2) 'Child'—(subject to Sched 1, para 16) a person under the age of 18.

(3) 'Child of the family'—in relation to the parties to a marriage:
    (a) a child of both those parties;
    (b) any other child, not being a child who is placed with those parties as foster parents by a local authority or voluntary organisation, who has been treated by both of those parties as a child of their family.

(4) 'Contact order'—this is a 'section 8' order (*see below*) but is not specifically dealt with within the scope of this book.

(5) 'Family proceedings'—for the purposes of the CA 1989, means any proceedings:
    (a) under the inherent jurisdiction of the High Court in relation to children; and
    (b) under the enactments as set out in CA 1989, s 8(4): CA 1989, s 8(3).

(6) 'Parental responsibility'—all the rights, duties, powers, responsibilities and authority which by law a parent has in relation to the child and his property: CA 1989, s 3.

(7) 'Parental responsibility agreement'—an agreement in prescribed form made by the father and mother of a child in accordance with CA 1989, s 4.

(8) 'Prohibited steps order'—an order that no step which could be taken by a parent in meeting his parental responsibility for a child, and which is of a kind specified in the order, shall be taken by any person without the consent of the court: CA 1989, s 8(1).

(9) 'Residence order'—an order settling the arrangements to be made as to the person with whom a child is to live: CA 1989, s 8(1).

(10) 'Section 8 order'—includes a residence order and a specific issue order, and any order which varies or discharges them: CA 1989, s 8(2).

(11) 'Specific issue order'—an order giving direction for the purpose of determining a specific question which has arisen, or may arise, in connection with any aspect of parental responsibility for a child: CA 1989, s 8(1).

For the purposes of this chapter a father of a child not married to the child's mother at the time of his birth is referred to as 'an unmarried father'.

Parental responsibility

There is no further elucidation in the CA 1989 of what 'those rights, powers . . .' etc might be, but it can generally be taken to include the right and power for a person with parental responsibility to change a child's name.

A range of persons can have parental responsibility, either 'automatically' or acquired under the provisions of the CA 1989. It is an important starting point to know whether or not a person attempting to change a child's name formally or informally does in fact have parental responsibility, and indeed whether anyone has an obligation not to change, or even to take steps to prevent an attempted change taking place.

The following pages contain a resume of the CA 1989 provisions relating to acquisition, retention and loss of parental responsibility.

Acquisition

The following persons have or can acquire parental responsibility:

Mother

A mother has automatic parental responsibility for her child from the time of its birth, whether or not she was married to the father of the child at that time: CA 1989, s 2(1) and (2). If she was not married at the time of the child's birth, the nature and quality of her parental responsibility is not diminished by her subsequent marriage to the child's father, nor indeed any other man. *See* CA 1989, s 2(5) which states that more than one person may have parental responsibility for the same child at the same time; and also CA 1989, s 2(6) which states that a person having parental responsibility does not lose it because someone else acquires it with respect to the same child.

The mother's separation or divorce from the father, whether or not she was married to him at the time of the birth, does not affect the nature and quality of her parental responsibility, unless her rights and obligations are restricted in any way by court order.

Father

If the child's father was married to the mother at the time of the child's birth he, like the mother, has automatic parental responsibility, and the provisions applicable to the mother as set out *above* apply also to him.

If the child's father was not married to the mother at the time of the birth then he can only acquire parental responsibility under some provision of the CA 1989: CA 1989, s 2(2). If the father subsequently marries the mother, then he acquires parental responsibility by virtue of the marriage: *see* CA 1989, s 2(3) and the Family Law Reform Act 1987, s 1.

A father is no longer deemed to be the natural guardian of his legitimate child, that rule having been abolished by CA 1989, s 2(4).

However, it should be noted that even if the father does not have parental responsibility for the child but does have the care of him, then he can (subject to the provisions of the Act) do what is reasonable in the case for the purpose of safeguarding or promoting the child's welfare. *See* CA 1989, s 3(5) which could conceivably include changing the child's name for a particular purpose (although this section may have more relevance and practical application in cases where the child is in the temporary care of, eg a teacher). *See* p 75 for the meaning of 'welfare'.

An unmarried father, whether or not he lives with the child's mother, or in the same household as the child (without having been granted parental responsibility by virtue of a residence order in his favour), may acquire parental responsibility in addition to the mother under CA 1989, s 4. This section deals with parental responsibility orders and parental responsibility agreements.

He *must* have a parental responsibility order made in his favour if the court grants him a residence order, but he does not automatically lose it when the residence order is no longer in force. By virtue of CA 1989, s 12(4) he cannot in any event lose the parental responsibility at any time while the particular residence order is in force.

Section 91(7) of the CA 1989 states that any order made under CA 1989, s 4(1) shall continue in force until the child reaches the age of 18 unless it is brought to an end earlier.

If there is no parental responsibility order (which includes one made in connection with a residence order) or agreement under CA 1989 s 4, then an unmarried father has no parental responsibility umbrella under which he is free to change his child's name. It is of course possible, but it is probably unlikely in practice, that he could bring about an unopposed informal change in the child's name by causing the change to take place by use and reputation.

An unmarried father may:

(a) apply to the court for an order giving him parental responsibility for his child: CA 1989, s 4(1)(a); or

(b) make a formal agreement, called a parental responsibility agreement, with the mother: CA 1989 s 4(1)(b).

Note that this will only have effect if made in accordance with any prescribed regulations, currently the Parental Responsibility Agreement Regulations 1991 (SI No 1478), as amended by the Parental Responsibility Agreement (Amendment) Regulations 1994 (SI No 3157).

A parental responsibility agreement continues in force until the child reaches the age of 18 or it is brought to an end earlier: CA 1989, s 91(8).

An unmarried father could apply to the court to be appointed the child's guardian under CA 1989 s 5(1) if, eg the mother having died, the child then has no parent with parental responsibility for him. Alternatively the court, in any family proceedings before it, could appoint him the guardian on its own volition under CA 1989, s 5(2). The child's mother could appoint the father to become the child's guardian in the event of her death: CA 1989, s 5(3), and as guardian he would in that capacity acquire parental responsibility when the appointment took effect.

Non-parental spouse

Whether as a wife or a husband, a non-parental spouse does not acquire any parental responsibility for a child simply by marriage to the child's mother or father. However, parental responsibility could be acquired on adopting a child, by becoming a guardian, or becoming a person in whose favour a residence order is granted.

Guardians

As from 14 October 1991, a guardian of a child can only be appointed in accordance with the provisions of the CA 1989: CA 1989, s 5(13). A guardian will have parental responsibility when the appointment takes effect: CA 1989, s 5(7) and (8).

Guardian appointed by the court If any person makes a court application with respect to a child the court has power to appoint that person to be the child's guardian. However, this will only be the case if the child does not have a parent with parental responsibility for the child, or there is a residence order in favour of a child's parent or guardian who has died while the order is in force: CA 1989, s 5(1)(*a*) and (*b*). As to residence orders generally *see below* at p 71. An order under CA 1989, s 5(1)(*a*) continues in force until the child reaches 18 unless brought to an end earlier.

The court can of its own volition, in any family proceedings, appoint a person to be a child's guardian, even though there has been no application in this particular respect: CA 1989, s 5(2).

Guardian appointed by a parent A parent with parental responsibility can appoint, solely or jointly, another person to be a guardian of a child in the event of the appointor's death: CA 1989, s 5(3), and *see* s 5(10) as to joint appointments.

Guardian appointed by an existing guardian or guardians An existing guardian (or guardians) can appoint, solely or jointly, another person to become the guardian of a child in the event in the guardian's death: CA 1989, s 5(4), and *see* s 5(10) as to joint appointments.

Guardianship appointments under CA 1989, s 5(3) and (4) are only valid if they comply with the conditions laid down in CA 1989, s 5(5)(*a*) and (*b*). *See also* CA 1989, s 5(7) and (8) as to when an appointment under CA 1989, s 5(3) or (4) actually takes effect. Appointments by parents or guardians, where there is no residence order in force, take effect immediately on the death of those persons where a child is left without a parent with parental responsibility for him: CA 1989, s 5 (7)(*a*). If on the death of the appointor the child is still left with a parent with parental responsibility for him the guardianship only takes effect on the death of that second parent.

Where a current residence order in favour of the appointing parent or guardian was in force immediately before his death the guardianship appointment takes effect on the death of the appointor, whether or not the child has a surviving parent with parental responsibility for him: CA 1989, s 5(7)(*b*) (except if the residence order was also made in favour or a surviving parent: CA 1989, s 5(9)).

As stated *above* at p 67, where there is a current residence order in favour of a parent or guardian who has died, the court can appoint any individual to be a guardian: CA 1989, s 5(1)(*b*) (except where the residence order was made in favour of the surviving parent: CA 1989, s 5(9)).

Section 6 of the CA 1989 deals with the revocation and disclaimer of guardianship appointments under CA 1989, s 5 (3) and (4), and the position will need to be checked before proceeding to advise a guardian whether or not he has power to change a child's name. It must be remembered that an original appointment may not have been revoked, but an additional appointment made.

If guardianship is disclaimed then the disclaimer is of no effect unless recorded in the manner laid down in any current regulations and a change of the child's name will be validly carried out until such time as the disclaimer takes effect.

The court has an overriding power to curtail the appointment of any guardian on the application of anyone else who has parental responsibility for the child, or indeed, the child himself with the leave of the court, or in any family proceedings if the court thinks fit without a separate application having been made: CA 1989, s 6(7). Loss of guardianship status will mean a loss of parental responsibility unless the guardian already had or acquires parental responsibility under some other provision of the CA 1989.

Surrogate mothers
Note should be made of the position under the Surrogacy Arrangements Act 1985. By virtue of s 1(2) a surrogate mother means a woman who carries a child in pursuance of an arrangement made both before she began to carry the child and with a view to the child being handed over, and the parental responsibility being met (so far as is practicable) by

another person or persons. She does not appear to lose her parental responsibility as no surrogacy arrangement is enforceable by or against any of the persons making it: Surrogacy Arrangements Act 1985, s 1A.

Human Fertilisation and Embryology Act 1990
Parental responsibility may be acquired as a result of the application of the Human Fertilisation and Embryology Act 1990 ('HFEA 1990'), and where by virtue of ss 27 or 28 a person is treated as a mother or father of a particular child then she or he is treated in law as the mother or father of the child for all purposes: HFEA 1990, s 29.

Mother Where a woman has carried a child as a result of having placed in her an embryo, or sperm and eggs, then she and no other woman is to be treated as the mother of the child (subject only to the provisions relating to adoption): HFEA 1990, s 27, and she will have automatic parental responsibility.

Father Where at the time of placing in a married woman an embryo, or sperm and eggs, or her artificial insemination, and the creation of the embryo was not brought about with her husband's sperm, her husband is treated as the child's father unless it is shown that he did not consent to the placing in her of the embryo, or sperm and eggs, or her artificial insemination: HFEA 1990, s 28(2).

Because he is treated as the child's father and is married to the mother at the time of the birth he will have automatic parental responsibility for the child in question. However, a man treated as the father of the child but not married to the mother, will not have automatic parental responsibility for the child but can only acquire it in accordance with the provisions of the CA 1989.

Where a man is treated as the child's father under HFEA 1990, s 28 then no other man is to be treated as the father or the child: HFEA 1990, s 28(4).

The court has power under HFEA 1990, s 30 to make a 'parental order' in certain circumstances.

Third parties

Consistent with the principle that parental responsibility can be shared (*see* CA 1989, s 2), someone (not necessarily the mother or father) who already has parental responsibility for a child may arrange for some or all of it to be met by one or more persons acting on his behalf: CA 1989, s 2(9). This can be, but is not necessarily, someone who already has parental responsibility for the child: CA 1989, s 2(10).

The Act does not specify how the arrangement is to be made, or if it is to be formal or informal, but an application to the court to endorse the arrangement or the creation of a power of attorney would be sufficient evidence. Such an arrangement does not absolve the person making it from any liability he would otherwise incur, arising from any failure to meet any part of his parental responsibility for the child in question: CA 1989, s 2(11). It does not seem that this person has automatic parental responsibility, or that he acquires any under the terms of the Act.

Where a court makes a residence order, then the person (not being a parent or guardian) in whose favour the order is made will acquire parental responsibility while that residence order is in force: CA 1989, s 12(2). An unmarried father can acquire parental responsibility by virtue of this section as the court must make a 'parental responsibility' order at the same time in his favour. The parental responsibility acquired under that order will continue until the child reaches 18 or it is brought to an end.

The following may also acquire parental responsibility:

A *local authority* cannot acquire parental responsibility with a residence order as it may not apply for such on order or indeed have one made in its favour: CA 1989, s 9, but it will acquire it by virtue of a care order being made in its favour: CA 1989, s 33(3), and *see* the position as to interim orders: CA 1989, s 38.

An *applicant for an emergency protection order* has parental responsibility for the child concerned while the order is in force: CA 1989, s 44(4), but note CA 1989, s 46(9) which states that where a child is in police protection neither the constable concerned nor the designated officer has parental responsibility for the child.

A *child's adoptive parents*: *see* Adoption Act 1976, s 12(1) and Chapter 6.

Loss of parental responsibility

A person may lose his parental responsibility in the following circumstances:

(1) By virtue of CA 1989, s 33(3)(*b*), a local authority with a care order in its favour has the power (where it is satisfied that it is necessary to do so in order to promote or safeguard a child's welfare) to determine the extent to which a parent or guardian may meet their parental responsibility. This is, however, subject to the proviso in s 33(5) that a local authority cannot prevent a parent or guardian who has care of a child from doing anything reasonable to safeguard the child's welfare.

(2) An unmarried father may lose any acquired parental responsibility by court order made on the application of anyone having parental responsibility for the child or, with leave, on the application of the child himself. This applies if the parental responsibility was acquired by agreement or order: CA 1989, s 4(3), (4).

(3) On revocation and disclaimer of guardianship: *see generally* CA 1989, s 6 and s 6 (7) as to the circumstances in which the guardianship can be brought to an end by the court.

(4) On the expiry of a residence order made in favour of someone not the parent or guardian of the child: CA 1989, s 12(2).

(5) Where the child is freed for adoption or is adopted.

(6) Where a parental order is made under HFEA 1990, s 30.

Statutory restrictions on changing a child's name

There are two specific statutory restrictions on changing a child's surname under the CA 1989. These are found in ss 13 and 33, and determine the position when there is either a residence order or a care order in force with respect to the child. Note the position regarding interim orders and the variation and discharge of orders. *See below* at p 73.

Residence order

No one may cause a child to be known by a new surname where there is a residence order in force with respect to that child, without either the written consent of every person who has parental responsibility for the child or the leave of the court: CA 1989, s 13(1). This appears to cover both informal and formal changes of surname. It does not apply to changes or attempted changes of Christian or other forenames.

The section clearly states that 'no person may . . . cause the child to be known by a new surname', and that means no one. The category is not restricted. There is no statutory obligation on anyone who has parental responsibility, nor indeed anyone else, to take steps to prevent the acquisition and use of a new surname, and it would be a question in every case as to whether a person who was aware of a change (actual or proposed) and who did nothing to prevent it, was acquiescing in the change to the extent that they were falling foul of s 13(1).

An application to the court for leave to change the child's name could be made where:

(a) it is simply not possible to obtain, for some practical reason, the required written consents; or

(b) there is an objection; or

(c) if, eg it was necessary to change the name in order to comply with a requirement in a will or settlement where someone else with parental responsibility might have personal reason to object.

It will be necessary for practitioners to ascertain if the residence order, interim or full, is actually in force or has been varied, discharged or simply expired. Note CA 1989, s 10 as to who can apply for a discharge or variation of the original order—this may include the child himself.

Unless there are exceptional circumstances a residence order cannot be made with respect to a child who has reached the age of 16, and again unless there are exceptional circumstances the order must expire when the child reaches the age of 16: CA 1989, s 9(6) and (7). Of course an original order could have been varied to extend its period to the child's 18th birthday.

If a deed poll evidencing a change of a child's name is to be enrolled (*see* Chapter 7 at p 94) then it will be noted that, if the child in question is aged 16 or more, he must endorse his consent on the deed poll, and could conceivably refuse to do so.

A residence order will automatically cease to have effect if, as a result of the order, the child lives or is to live with one of two parents (both of whom have parental responsibility for him) and the parents actually live together for a continuous period of more then six months: CA 1989, s 11(5).

A residence order will be discharged by the making of a care order, and the terms of CA 1989, s 33 will have effect for the duration of that order: CA 1989, s 91.

There is no provision in the CA 1989 to cover the case where a change of a child's name is desired, the child's parents are separated, but there is no residence order in force. In the absence of agreement, the appropriate course seems to be to obtain a court order: *see* Hershman and Mcfarlane *Children: Law & Practice* (Jordan & Sons 1991), vol 1 A [13].

Opposition to a change of the child's name would form the basis for an application for a prohibited steps order and/or a specific issue order.

Care order

While a care order is in force with respect to a child, again no one may cause the child to be known by a new surname without either the written consent of every person who has parental responsibility for the child, or the leave of the court: CA 1989, s 33(7), and *see* the similar provision regarding residence orders *above* at pp 71–2. The local authority has parental responsibility for the child while the care order is in force and could itself withhold consent for a change of name: but note CA 1989, s 33(3)(*b*), (4) and (5) as *above* at p 70.

Section 33(7) of the CA 1989 states that '. . . no person may . . .', but the words 'authority', or 'local authority designated' are not used as throughout the rest of the section. However, it is submitted that they must be intended to be included in the section, as to exclude them would give the authority *carte blanche* to change a child's name without consents or the leave of the court. That would also mean that another person seeking to change the name of a child in care could proceed to do so without the consent of the authority: *see* CA 1989, s 33(7). *See also Re J (A Minor) (Change of Name)* [1993] 1 FLR 699.

Interim care orders

An interim care order may be made under CA 1989, s 38(1) and will have effect for whatever period of time is stated in the order. It will, in any event, cease to have any effect on whichever of certain events first occurs, eg the expiry of eight weeks from the date on which the order is made: *see* CA 1989, s 38(4). Practitioners will need to take care to check if the interim order has in fact ceased to have effect in the particular instance.

Care orders may be discharged by the court on the application of anyone with parental responsibility, or the local authority designated by the order or even the child himself. Another order may be substituted, eg a supervision order, under which there is no statutory restriction on change of name. However, note that if a residence order is substituted then the statutory restriction on change of name will continue in the same form but under the different section of the Act.

A care order is discharged on the making of a residence order: CA 1989, s 91(1). A care order other than an interim care order continues in force until the child reaches the age of 18, unless brought to an end earlier: CA 1989, s 91(12).

An existing care order has effect subject to the provisions of any emergency protection order under CA 1989, s 44.

Anyone seeking to prevent the change of a child's name would apply to the court for a prohibited steps order and / or a specific issue order.

Prevention of a change of a child's name where there is no statutory restriction

It will be recalled that, except in the circumstances outlined *above* where there are statutory restrictions on the change of a child's surname, anyone who has parental responsibility for a child has the right and power to change the child's forename or surname, whether or not evidencing the change by document evidence, and without recourse to any other person or persons with parental responsibility: CA 1989, s 2(7), However, this does not mean that those other persons have no right to object to a change (actual or proposed), and the child himself also has a right of action. Note though the *Practice Direction* at Appendix B.

In the case of any dispute a court order should be sought. It is possible to apply for a 'section 8' prohibited steps order or specific issue order. Though these are normally made in connection with divorce proceedings, they are not restricted to such, and are available in other instances as free standing applications: *see* CA 1989, s 10(1). This section states: 'In *any* family proceedings in which a question arises with respect to the *welfare* of any child the court may make a section 8 order . . .' (italics supplied). *See also* CA 1989, s 10(2) which states: 'The court may also make a section 8 order with respect to any child on the application of a person who . . .' and then sets out the persons who may apply.

There is a range of persons entitled to make an application for a prohibited steps order or a specific issue order, which includes parents, guardians and anyone in whose favour a residence order is in force with respect to the child in question. It also includes anyone who under either s 10(1) or (2) has obtained the leave of the court to make the application.

Where it is the child himself who seeks leave to make an application for a prohibited steps or a specific issue order, then the court may only grant leave if it is satisfied that the child has sufficient understanding to make the proposed application: CA 1989, s 10(8). Each case would have to be individually assessed by the court, which could call for a welfare report on the issue: *see* CA 1989, s 7.

In any other case where leave is sought then the court must, in deciding whether or not to grant leave, have particular regard to:
 (a) the nature of the proposed application;
 (b) the applicant's connection with the child;
 (c) any risk that the child's life would be harmed by disruption to the child's life as a result of the application.

For children in care the court must have regard to the authority's plans for the child's future and the wishes and feelings of the child's parents: *see* CA 1989, s 10(9).

Section 8 order

A section 8 prohibited steps order or a specific issue order may contain directions about how it is to be put into effect and/or it may impose conditions which must be complied with: *see* CA 1989, s 11(7). For example, it is possible that a condition might be imposed to evidence a change of name by formal deed poll and enrol the change at the Supreme Court within a certain time limit. The orders or any of the provisions can also be made to have effect for a specified period and the court can make any additional, supplementary or consequential provisions as it thinks fit.

No court can make such an order which is to have effect for a period which will end after the child has reached the age of 16 unless it is satisfied that the circumstances of the case are exceptional. Nor can a court make such an order other than one varying or discharging such an order with respect to a child who has reached the age of 16 unless it is satisfied that the circumstances of the case are exceptional: CA 1989, s 9(6) and (7). *See also* CA 1989, s 91(10) and (11) as to the duration of orders.

Welfare of the child

The overriding principle is that the child's welfare must be the court's paramount consideration when it determines any question with respect to the upbringing of a child: CA 1989, s 1(1)(*a*). This will apply whether it is the parties to a divorce or separation, any person with parental responsibility, or even the child himself who is bringing an application before the court.

The court has to have particular regard to the list of factors set out in CA 1989, s 1(3), when it considers:

(a) whether to make, vary or discharge a section 8 order, where any party to the proceedings opposes that making, variation or discharge; or

(b) whether to make, vary or discharge an order under CA 1989, Pt IV (ie care and supervision orders), which includes an order giving leave of the court for a person to cause a child to be known by a new surname.

The factors the court must consider are as follows:

(a) the ascertainable wishes and feelings of the child concerned (considered in the light of his age and understanding);

(b) his physical, emotional and educational needs;

(c) the likely effect on him of any change in his circumstances;

(d) his age, sex, background and any characteristics of his which the court considers relevant;

(e) any harm which he has suffered or is at risk of suffering;

(f) how capable each of his parents, and any other person in relation to whom the court considers the question to be relevant, is of meeting his needs;

(g) the range of powers available to the court under the CA 1989 in the proceedings in question.

The list is not exhaustive, but in the particular circumstances outlined in s 1(4) *above* the court must pay particular regard to these matters, although but not necessarily in any order of preference. The judge must deal with each case on its own facts.

The court has power, when it considers any question with respect to a child under the CA 1989, to require and take account of any statement in, and any evidence given in, respect of the matters referred to in a welfare report under CA 1989, s 7(1).

Although the following cases were decided before the CA 1989 came into force, when the rule on the subject was laid down in the Guardianship of Minors Act 1971, s 1 (which stated the court had to have regard to the child's welfare as the first and paramount consideration), they are still relevant today in considering 'welfare'.

In *J v C* [1970] AC 668, at pp 710–711 Lord MacDermott gave a well-known explanatory passage. He said that the section meant more than that the child's welfare is to be treated as the top item in a list: all relevant facts, relationships, claims and wishes of parents, choices and other circumstances are to be considered, and that course followed which is most in the interest of the child's welfare.

In *W v A (Child: Surname)* [1981] 1 All ER 100 Dunn LJ cited this passage and translated it into terms appropriate to a disputed proposal to change a child's name after the divorce of his parents. It was a matter of discretion for the judge, after hearing the case, seeing the witnesses and parents and possibly the child, to decide whether such a change was in the child's interest. All the circumstances relevant to the particular case should be taken into account, including the possible embarrassment of the child at school, his long term interest, the importance of his link with the father's family, and the stability of the mother's new marriage.

These, indicated his Lordship, are but typical examples of the kinds of consideration which arise in these cases. In this case the mother and father were married in 1966 and had two children. After divorce both of the father and the mother remarried. There was joint custody of the children, the mother having care and control, the father reasonable access. The mother wished the children to use her second husband's surname, and the children, at the time aged 12 and 14, told the judge that they themselves wished to use it.

It was held that the change of a child's surname after divorce was an important issue to be decided in accordance with the Guardianship of Minors Act 1971, s 1 by reference to what was in the best interests of the child's welfare in the particular circumstances, that being the first and paramount consideration.

Dunn LJ held that he was faced with two conflicting lines of authority, the first being that the change of a child's surname is an important matter, not to be undertaken lightly, and the second that the change of a child's surname is a comparatively unimportant matter. Having reviewed the authorities, he chose to follow the first line and followed *Re W G* (1976) 6 Fam Law 210, where the gist of the decision was that neither the remarriage of the mother after divorce (with the consequent change, in practice, of her name) nor the administrative convenience of a school was sufficient to outweigh the longer term interests of a child, at all events if it could not be said that his father had failed to maintain a proper interest in him. The Court of Appeal thought that the difficulties in the relationship between the father and the child would increase if the latter ceased to bear the former's name.

Dunn LJ also referred to *R (BM) v R (DN) (Child: Surname)* [1978] 2 All ER 33 where the mother had left the father and their four children and had gone to live with a soldier at Bovington. Approximately two years later she obtained a decree nisi and custody of all four children. The youngest child C was unhappy and returned to live with her father. The real issue in the case was with whom the child should live and the question of the change of name arose only in this way. The other three children were known in the army camp as W, the soldier's surname.

In this case Stamp LJ said:

> I think that too much attention is paid to these matters of names of children . . . and it must be most convenient that they should be known as W in the camp in which they are being brought up where Sergeant W is the head of the family.

In *W v A (Child: Surname)* Dunn LJ said it was important not to take this out of context, or to take it as laying down any general proposition as to changes of name. In *R (BM) v R (DN) (Child: Surname) above*, Ormrod J referred to the change of name as a peripheral matter and no doubt in that case it was. He made general observations on the changing of surnames of children and emphasised the embarrassment for school authorities if children are not known by the same name as their mother. Dunn LJ thought these observations were clearly obiter and not necessary for the decision in *W v A (Child: Surname)*.

He also referred to but did not follow *D v B (otherwise D) (Child: Surname)* [1979] 1 All ER 92. At the end of the day in this case the question of the name was not in issue; the main issue being access. Ormrod J made some general remarks about changing names at p 100:

> What is real is that the father and the child should know one another, that the child should, in the course of time, come to recognise the fact that D is his natural father, and so long as that is understood, names are really of little

importance, and they only become important when they become a *casus belli* between the parents.

Dunn LJ in the present case, *W v A*, considered that these remarks were obiter, but even if necessary for the case they were in direct conflict with the dicta of Cairns LJ in *Re W G* (1976) 6 Fam Law 210.

In *L v F* (1978) *The Times*, 1 August Latey J held that the direct issue was whether the mother should or should not be allowed to change her children's surname to that of her new husband. He said:

> Until the two recent decisions of Ormrod and Stamp LJJ the prevailing view as in *Re W G* and which had never been questioned was that, on a failure of a marriage, a decision to change children's names should never be taken unilaterally, and unless parents were in agreement, a decision about the matter should be approached by the courts as a matter of real importance.

The fact that one approach had been evolved over many years and the other had only recently been expressed did not mean either had to be accepted automatically as correct. Latey J thought the decision in *Re W G* was the correct one. A marriage could be dissolved but not the parenthood. The parents in most cases continued to play an important role in their children's emotional lives and development.

From the point of view of the children's best interests it was essential that the parents' feelings should be taken carefully and anxiously into consideration. He rejected a remarried mother's suggestion that it would add to her children's sense of security if they were to be known by her new name. The children might grow to resent having been deprived of their father's name, at a time when they did not understand the matter and had no say in it.

In *W v A* Dunn LJ said that:

> As in all cases concerning the future of children whether they be custody, access, education or, as in this case, the change of a child's name, s 1 of the Guardianship of Minors Act 1971 requires that the court shall regard 'the welfare of the [child] as the first and paramount consideration'.

He referred to the fact that in *J v C* [1969] 1 All ER 788 at p 820 Lord McDermott said 'they must mean more than that the child's welfare is to be treated as the top item in a list of items relevant to the matter in question'. *See above* at p 76.

It is a matter for the individual judge to decide in each particular set of circumstances whether a name should be changed, and the judge will take into account all the circumstances of the case, including both the embarrassment which may be caused to the child by not changing his name, and the long-term interests and importance of maintaining the child's links with his paternal or maternal family. In the present case he thought the judge at first instance correct. The children were too young to express an opinion on a fairly drastic step: 'I pay little regard to their views, which are views that largely reflect the mother's views'.

In *Re T (otherwise H) (An Infant)* [1963] Ch 238 the parents of a ten-year-old girl were divorced in 1959, the mother having custody, and the father access to the child by agreement. The father and mother both re-married in 1960. The mother subsequently executed a deed poll whereby she, purporting to act as legal guardian, renounced and abandoned the use of the infant's surname and declared that from the date of the deed poll the infant has assumed the mother's new surname. Buckley J held:

> One can imagine cases in which it might be in the interests of a child to cease to be known by a particular name, perhaps because of some particularly unhappy association which that name might have acquired or possibly in order to comply with some condition contained in some trust document.

But in the present case there was no such reason.

He went on to say that in the case of a divided family the aim of the court was to maintain the child's contact, respect and affection with and for its parents. To deprive a child of a father's name was not in the best interests of the child, because it was injurious to the link between the father and the child to suggest to the child that there is some reason why it is desirable that she should be called by some name other than her father's name. The fact of divorce was not sufficient.

See also Re McGrath (Infants) [1893] 1 Ch 143 per Lindley J:

> . . . the welfare of a child is not to be measured by money only, nor by physical comfort only. The word welfare must be taken in its widest sense . . . Nor can the ties of affection be disregarded.

See also Re E [1963] 3 All ER 874, a case regarding the adoption and religious upbringing of a child.

It seems clear, then, that a heavy onus rests on a mother who argues for a change in the name of her legitimate child unless the father consents. Encouragement for the traditional view against such a change has, per-haps, been shown by the legislature in its concern to preserve relationships after divorce: *see*, eg the former Adoption Act 1976, ss 14(3) and 15(4) (repealed by CA 1989, s 108(6), Sched 14, paras 1, 2 and 7, and Sched 15).

If in a particular case it can be shown that there is a special risk that a difference in name between a child and his mother would cause the child distress in the shape of 'ragging', or perhaps more serious mistreatment at the hands of his associates, that will be a factor to be considered. Also considered will be any unusual degree of inconvenience or confusion which the use of the father's name would cause. To evaluate these elements requires close acquaintance with the circumstances of the particular case, the age and resilience of the child, and the nature of his surroundings. Certainly, those who advance such considerations must show that the child is likely to suffer real discomfiture, distinct from the mere embarrassment of the mother. It is the welfare of the child that must be the first regard.

In *Re J (A Minor) (Change of Name)* [1993] 1 FLR 699 a child, who had been severely abused by her parents (who no longer knew her whereabouts), was living with foster parents and wished to use their name for some specific purposes. The local authority made an ex parte application in respect of J (who supported the application) and her foster parents. It was held that in the particular circumstances it could be very damaging for J if the parents were served with the application by the local authority, for them to re-enter her life and for her to know that they had been served with the application. The parents might be able to trace her whereabouts. As the application was that J use the foster parents' name for some purposes rather than make a 'legal' change, it was held that this particular application should be ex parte. However, Booth J also held at p 701 that it must only be in exceptional cases, when demanded by concern for a child's welfare, that an application for change of a child's surname should be made ex parte and without notice to the parents. It is interesting to note that in this case J was given leave to use her foster parents' name for the purposes of school, hospital, general practitioners, dentist and for everyday living purposes, the latter not being further defined. It seems the 'legal' change mentioned was probably a formal immediate change, whereas a change in this case was an authorised informal usage.

In *Re F (Child: Surname)* [1994] Fam Law 12 a divorced woman resumed her maiden name and obtained leave to change the surname of her two daughters aged five and three. The Court of Appeal held that the judge at first instance had failed to regard the change of name as a matter of importance and in this case there was nothing in a formal change of name that would be for the children's well-being.

It will be a matter for the judge in each case whether or not to grant leave for the change of a child's name.

Procedure

See generally The Family Court Practice 1995 (Jordan & Sons).

An application for leave to change a child's name under CA 1989, s 13 or s 33(7) should be made on Form C1 or C2 as appropriate; any order being made on form CHA 21. *See* the Family Proceedings Rules 1991 (SI No 1247), as amended by the Family Proceedings (Amendment)

Rules 1994 (SI No 808).

An application under CA 1989, s 33(7) must be commenced in the magistrates' court: *see* the Children (Allocation of Proceedings) Order 1991 (SI No 1677), art 3 as amended by the Children (Allocation of Proceedings) (Amendment) Order 1993 (SI No 624) (subject to exceptions set out therein). *See also Re J (A Minor) (Change of Name) above* where it was held that in exceptional cases involving an ex parte application for a change of surname, the application should be transferred to a higher court from the magistrates' court.

See the Family Proceedings Rules 1991 (SI No 1247), r 4.4 and the Family Proceedings Courts (Children Act 1989) Rules 1991 (SI No 1395), which govern the making of applications in the county courts, High Court and magistrates' courts, respectively. Otherwise, applications concerning children are not restricted to particular courts.

Chapter 6

Adoption and Registration of Births and Deaths

Adoption order

An adoption order is one made under the provisions of the Adoption Act 1976 (as amended), which gives parental responsibility for a child to the adopters. Those children who can be adopted are single, never having been married, and aged under 18 as at the date of making the order: Adoption Act 1976, s 5. A child may be adopted by a married couple or by one person: *see* Adoption Act 1976, ss 14 and 15.

Change of the child's name—welfare of the child

The adoptive parent or parents will usually wish to change the child's surname to their own, and may also decide to change his forename or forenames, although this will be less common. Alternatively, and especially with an older child of greater understanding, they may elect to continue to call the child by his pre-adoptive name or names, and the court must consider the child's views.

Each case will, of course, depend on its own facts. Indeed under the Adoption Act 1976, s 6 a court, in coming to any decision on a child's adoption (which will include a decision on a change of name), must give first consideration to the child's welfare. A court has a duty to ascertain the child's wishes and feelings about the decision, having regard to his age and understanding. Clearly, a court could reject an unsuitable forename—one, for instance, that having regard to the child's environment might expose him to more than a tolerable share of the ridicule of his schoolmates.

Parental responsibility

After adoption the new parent or parents have the normal rights, under their newly acquired parental responsibility, to change the child's name by the simple or more formal means described in this book.

In the past it was felt by some that adoption was too frequently used as a means of changing the surname of a child who passed, on the break up of a marriage and his mother's remarriage, into the charge of a step-father. *See eg Re D (Minors) (Adoption by Parent)* [1973] Fam 209 at p 216. Hence the enactment of the Adoption Act 1976, ss 14(3) and 15(4) (now repealed), requiring a court to prefer a custody order to an adoption order in circumstances of this kind.

Custody orders can no longer be made and under the Children Act 1989 ('CA 1989') parental responsibility remains with a father on the mother's remarriage. The father would lose his parental responsibility on the making of an adoption order, but only in the circumstances set out in the Adoption Act 1976, s 16, and which involve his agreement (except where this is dispensed with under s 16(2)).

Married parents and unmarried mothers will completely lose their parental responsibility if their child is freed for adoption under the Adoption Act 1976, s 18(5) (as amended by CA 1989, Sched 10, para 6(2)), or is adopted under the Adoption Act 1976, s 12. Under this Act parental responsibility will be respectively vested in the adoption agency or the adoptive parent or parents. The adoption order will also defeat the parental responsibility vested in *any* person before the order, and also any order made under the CA 1989: Adoption Act 1976, s 12(3) as inserted by CA 1989, s 88, Sched 10, para 3.

The circumstances in which more than one person may adopt a child are set out in the Adoption Act 1976, s 14(1), (1A) and (1B) as follows:

(a) where the applicants, neither of whom is one of the child's parents, are married and both husband and wife have attained the age of 21 years; or

(b) where either the husband or wife is the parent of the child and is at least 18 and his or her spouse is at least 21.

Procedure

In the Form of Originating Process for an Adoption Order, the applicants can propose that the child is to be known by a new surname and forename or forenames. The child's original, or former, surname and forenames as stated in the birth and perhaps a previous adoption certificate (which must be exhibited to the application) are also entered on the form. If the child's name has been changed since the date of the birth or previous adoption certificate then this should be recorded here in the application.

The Registrar General will record the adoption order, including any new name granted, in the Adopted Children Register in Southport (*see* Appendix D), and the child's birth certificate is replaced by the issue of an adoption certificate. The birth certificate will merely be noted with the word 'adopted' or 're-adopted'. Evidence of the new name will be constituted by a certified copy of the entry in the Register (*see* the Adoption Act 1976, s 50 and the Forms of Adoption Entry Regulations 1975 (SI No 1959)).

It will not often be possible to produce detailed evidence of the change of name because the records linking the Adopted Children Register with the Registers of Births are kept confidential except in certain circumstances. *See* the Adoption Act 1976, s 50(5), (6). However, a court may think fit in sufficiently serious or important circumstances, eg in order to establish title to a property, to order disclosure of the records.

An adopted person who has attained the age of 18 has a right of access to his birth record under s 51 of the Act.

See further Josling and Levy, *Adoption of Children* 10th edn (Longman 1985).

Births and Deaths Registration Acts

Where a birth is registered within three months from the date of birth of a child the Registrar must enter the name and surname of the child, and if a name is not given, then only the surname of the child. (Regulation 2 of the Registration of Births and Deaths Regulations 1987 (SI No 2088) (as amended) defines 'name' as not including surname.)

If a name is not given the Registrar enters the surname only.

The surname to be entered must be that which it is intended that the child will be known: *see* the 1987 Regulations, reg 9.

Where, before the expiration of 12 months from registration of its birth, the name by which any child was registered is altered (or if it was registered without a name, a name is given to the child) the Registrar having custody of the register containing the entry of birth is to make an entry in the register upon delivery to him of a certificate in the form prescribed in the Regulations: *see* the Births and Deaths Registration Act 1953, s 13. The forms differ depending on whether or not the child's name was altered or given in baptism. *See* the 1987 Regulations, reg 14 and forms 3 and 4 together with the Births, Deaths and Marriages Fees Order 1995 (SI No 3257).

Where the name has not been given or altered within 12 months of the first registration this procedure is not possible, but a statutory declaration can be made to the effect that the birth and baptismal certificates relate to the same child.

Except in cases where a re-registration is permitted, as set out *below*, or conceivably in the case of error (see the 1953 Act, s 29 and the 1987 Regulations, regs 53–61), there seems to be no provision for a change of surname to be noted in the register of births, though a child's surname is recorded on registration and indexed. Section 29(1) of the 1953 Act states that no register of births may be altered except as may be permitted by statute.

Section 10 of the 1953 Act (as substituted by the Family Law Reform Act 1987, s 24) sets out the evidence required to enable the father's name to be entered on the register when the birth is first registered of a child whose parents are not married to each other at its birth. However, this does not necessarily mean that the child must be registered as bearing that name. The child's surname could, of course, be changed by use and reputation or formally recorded by way of deed poll. *See* the 1953 Act, s 10 for full details of the evidence required. For declarations and changes to prescribed forms *see* the Registration of Births and Deaths (Amendment) Regulations 1994 (SI No 1948).

Re-registration of birth

Re-registration under any of the following provisions may, and probably will, result in a change of a recorded surname:

(1) Section 10A of the 1953 Act (as inserted by the Family Law Reform Act 1987, s 25 and amended by CA 1989, Sched 12, para 6) enables the recording of the father's name in cases where the original registration was of an illegitimate birth showing no father's name. An initiating request is necessary and this may be submitted by the parents jointly, or by one of them supported by:
   (a) a statutory declaration;
   (b) a certified copy of a parental responsibility agreement or parental responsibility order under CA 1989, s 4; and
   (c) a certified copy of any order as listed in the 1953 Act, s 10(1), (1A).

The child's consent, if he is over 16, may be required.

(2) Section 14 of the 1953 Act (augmented by the Legitimacy Act 1976, s 11(1) and Sched 1, para 6) allows the re-registration of the births of persons recognised by English law as having become legitimated by the subsequent marriage of their parents. *See* the

Registration of Births and Deaths (Amendment) Regulations 1994 (SI No 1948) as to amendments to prescribed forms.

(3) Section 14A of the 1953 Act (as inserted by the Family Law Reform Act 1987, s 26) enables the re-registration of a birth after a declaration of parentage under the Family Law Act 1986, s 56 (as substituted by the Family Law Reform Act 1987, s 22).

Chapter 7

Deeds Poll

General

A deed poll is a commonly-used and convenient formal means of evidencing a change of name whether it be of a surname, forename or Christian name. For the latter *see below* at p 97. For suggested forms *see* Appendix A.

Many persons will be content with the formality provided by the nature of the deed in itself, which will be acceptable for most practical purposes. However, it is important that practitioners should comply with the conditions set out *below* as to the form and contents of a deed poll, as required by the current enrolment regulations, should the client decide to have it enrolled at a later date.

The provisions of the current regulations relating to the enrolment of deeds poll, together with a brief summary of the relevant law relating to the nationality conditions contained in the regulations, are set out *below* at p 89 et seq.

Option to enrol

In order to provide proof of execution of the deed a Commonwealth citizen, as defined by the British Nationality Act 1981, s 37(1), may apply to have it enrolled in the Filing and Record Department of the Central Office of the Supreme Court (*see* RSC Ord 63, r 10). *See below* at p 96 as to aliens and p 109 as to the practice and procedure of the College of Arms on enrolment.

The enrolment of a deed does not confer additional legality, but it is proof that the court has checked and approved the deed according to the regulations for enrolment, currently the Enrolment of Deeds (Change of Name) Regulations 1994 (SI No 604). For fees as from 1 February 1995 *see* Appendix D.

Although there will be many instances when some formal proof of perfection of a change of name is required (eg when dealing with the Passport Office or the Land Registry), deeds poll are not required or even authorised by law to be enrolled. The main purposes of enrolment are safe custody, availability of copies and advertisement of the change of name in the *London Gazette*.

Application to enrol is optional and, if made, there is no time limit within which the deed must be enrolled. Enrolment is a matter within the ultimate discretion of the Senior Master of the Queen's Bench, as Head (under the Master of the Rolls) of the Filing Department, who will personally consider unusual kinds of application. His adverse decision may be referred to the Master of the Rolls for a final ruling. *See* the report of a case ((1979) *The Daily Telegraph*, 1 August, p 3), where Lord Denning MR, while emphasising the enhancing effect of enrolment, went on to say that refusal to enrol did not prevent the use of the name in question. Here Lord Denning declined to accept an application to enrol the addition of 'Lord de Carmel' to the applicant's name.

No express provision exists in the 1994 Regulations for cancelling the enrolment of a deed, but there is no doubt that the court may declare a deed to be ineffective: *Re T (otherwise H) (An Infant)* [1963] Ch 238. In this case a mother who had remarried executed a deed poll whereby she renounced and abandoned the use of her child's surname and declared that from the date of the deed the child had assumed the mother's new surname. Buckley J, holding 'there is no magic in a deed poll', went on to declare the deed poll ineffective in the circumstances of the case.

In *D v B (otherwise D) (Child: Surname)* [1978] 3 WLR 573 a mother, married in 1970, formed an attachment in 1975 to another man with whom she went to live, having become pregnant by her husband. On leaving her husband she executed a deed poll for herself and her children. It did not comply with the regulations then in force, which had to be complied with if the deed were to be enrolled (although no attempt was made to enrol it). On appeal it was held that since at common law a surname is merely a name by which a person is generally known, and the effect of a deed poll is merely evidential and had no other effect, the mother could not be required to execute a fresh deed poll. Also the deed poll made was not vitiated by the fact it did not comply with the regulations since:

(a) compliance was only required where it was intended to enrol the deed poll;

(b) a deed poll was effective whether enrolled or not; and

(c) there were no regulations governing the execution of deeds poll.

The sole effect of the failure to comply with the then (1949) regulations was that the deed poll could not be enrolled. It was held that the direction to execute a fresh deed poll given at first instance was unenforceable. In this type of case, if an order were properly made for the amendment of a deed which had been enrolled, the Senior Master would clearly have power to order the enrolled deed, and any copies issued, to be noted accordingly. Subject to such an order, cancellation could more simply be effected by means of a fresh deed reversing the change made by the earlier one.

Requirements for enrolment

Generally

A deed for enrolment may be typed or written by hand. No witnesses are required (*see below* at p 93) though it is a sensible precaution to have two, particularly where the deed involves the change of name of a child.

Personal attendance at the Filing and Record Department when making an application for enrolment is possible but not necessary. *See* Appendix D for addresses and current fees.

The 1994 Regulations

The Enrolment of Deeds (Change of Name) Regulations 1994 (SI No 604) ('the 1994 Regulations') came into force on 1 April 1994. They supersede previous regulations and govern the enrolment in the Central Office of the Supreme Court of deeds evidencing change of name (referred to in the Regulations as 'deeds poll'): the 1994 Regulations, reg 1.

Citizenship

The 'applicant', ie the person seeking to enrol the deed poll, must be a Commonwealth citizen as defined by the British Nationality Act 1981, s 37(1): the 1994 Regulations, reg 2(1) (read with regs 4 and 5 *below* as to residence).

If the applicant is a British citizen, a British Dependent Territories citizen or a British Overseas citizen, he must be so described in the deed poll. The deed poll must also specify under which section of the British Nationality Act 1981 he acquired his citizenship: the 1994 Regulations, reg 2(2). In any other case he must be described as a Commonwealth citizen: the 1994 Regulations, reg 2(3).

It is important that the applicant's citizenship (and indeed residence— *see below* at p 91 et seq) are carefully investigated (whether or not initially it is intended to enrol the deed). These matters are crucial, and are relevant in defining the jurisdiction which the court assumes when it enrols the deed and gives it judicial recognition.

The legality of the applicant's residence in the United Kingdom is important as the court must not be seen to endorse inferentially any infringement of immigration law.

The British Nationality Act 1981 defines the terms used in the 1994 Regulations, reg 2 and the relevant provisions are set out *below* at p 77 et seq.

Describing the citizenship of applicant under the 1994 Regulations, reg 2 for purposes of enrolment

To take what will be a common example for many years to come, a deed executed by a person who was a citizen of the United Kingdom and Colonies on 31 December 1982, with a right to reside in the United Kingdom, will describe that person as a British citizen by virtue of the British Nationality Act 1981, s 11. There are many other possibilities, and the circumstances of the individual to whom they relate must be considered when the deed is drafted in the light of the various sections of the British Nationality Act 1981 (and the provisions relating to British Nationals (Overseas)).

In the instances set out in (b) at p 97 and 'British Subjects' at p 105, the applicant must simply be described as a Commonwealth citizen, and there will be no need to refer to any section of the Act other than British Nationality Act 1981, s 37.

The descriptions 'British . . . by birth' or '. . . by descent' are used selectively in the British Nationality Act 1981 so as to refer only to those persons who were born after the Act's commencement on 1 January 1983. Yet in everyday speech they may be used loosely of British citizens, etc who, in the terms of the Act, 'acquired' that status at 1 January 1983 under, eg the British Nationality Act 1981, ss 11, 23, or 30. The writer understands that the colloquial descriptions are accepted in deeds presented for enrolment, provided that the appropriate section of the Act is specified in accordance with the 1994 Regulations, reg 2(2).

See below at p 91 for the documents which must be supplied on an application to register the deed poll in order to prove the citizenship claimed.

Marital status

The applicant must be described in the deed poll as single, married, widowed or divorced: the 1994 Regulations, reg 2(4) and *see* again *below* for the documents to be supplied with the application for registration.

Proof of citizenship, marriage, etc

The 1994 Regulations, reg 3(1) provide that as proof of the citizenship stated in the deed poll, the applicant must produce:

    (a) a birth certificate; or

    (b) a certificate of citizenship by registration or naturalisation or otherwise; or

    (c) some other documentary evidence.

Where birth (or adoption) certificates are lodged, the full form giving particulars of natural or adoptive parentage is preferable. However, the shortened form prescribed under the Births and Deaths Registration Act 1953, s 33 may be sufficient.

Married applicants

In addition to the documents set out in reg 3(1) *above*, a married applicant must:

    (a) produce his marriage certificate; and

    (b) show that notice of his intention to apply for the enrolment of the deed poll has been given to his spouse by delivery or by post to his spouse's last known address; and

    (c) show that he has obtained his spouse's consent to the proposed change of name or that there is good reason that the spouse's consent should be dispensed with.

A form for the spouse's consent is suggested at Appendix A, p 118.

Where application is made for the spouse's consent to be dispensed with, an affidavit by the applicant is required, and must include the following statements:

    (a) the reason for taking the new name unless, in the case of a woman, she is resuming her maiden surname;

    (b) if the applicant is cohabiting with a man (or woman) whose name she (or he) is taking, a statement as to:

        (i)   whether that man or woman has a wife or husband;

        (ii) where precisely the spouse is living; and

        (iii) whether the man or woman whose name is being taken is separated or divorced from the spouse;

(c) if the applicant is cohabiting with a man or woman other than his
     or her spouse, a statement as to whether there are any children:
     (i)   of the marriage of that man or woman;
     (ii) of the marriage of the applicant; or
     (iv) born to the applicant and the person with whom he or she is
           cohabiting.
     If there are any such children, the affidavit should state their ages
     and whereabouts, and who has parental responsibility for them
     (as to parental responsibility *see* Chapter 5);
(d) that notice of intention to apply for enrolment of the deed (with
     a definite and formal request for his or her consent) has been given
     to the applicant's spouse by delivery or by post to his or her last
     known address, and that consent has been refused. If it is not
     known where the spouse is living, the affidavit must describe the
     steps which have been taken to trace him or her;
(e) any other relevant information; and
(f) a request for leave to dispense with the spouse's consent.
Copies of any correspondence relevant under (d) must be exhibited.

Statutory declaration

The deed poll and the documents referred to in the 1994 Regulations,
reg 3 *above* must be exhibited to a statutory declaration made by a
Commonwealth citizen who is (and who must declare in the declaration
that he is) a householder in the United Kingdom. The declaration must
state the period during which the householder has known the applicant,
which should ordinarily not be less than ten years, and must identify the
person referred to in the documents exhibited to the statutory declaration
as the applicant: the 1994 Regulations, reg 4(2).

If the period stated in reg 4(2) is less than ten years, the Master of the
Rolls may call for the applicant to provide further information, and has
an absolute discretion as to whether to allow enrolment of the deed poll
at all: the 1994 Regulations, reg 4(3). A form of statutory declaration is
suggested *below* at Appendix A.

Residence of applicant outside United Kingdom

An applicant, resident outside the United Kingdom, must provide
evidence that his absence is not intended to be permanent. He may be
required to produce a solicitor's certificate as to the nature and probable
duration of such residence: the 1994 Regulations, reg 5. It is understood
that the period must not usually exceed three years, but it is obviously

advisable to check the current position with the Filing and Record Department. The regulation allows for the case of an applicant, eg who is fulfilling a comparatively short service contract abroad, pursuing a course of foreign studies, or posted abroad as a member of the armed forces.

Signature of deed poll

Except where the applicant is a child under the age of 16, he must sign the deed poll in both his old and new names: the 1994 Regulations, reg 6 and *see* reg 8(4) at pp 94–96.

Enrolment

Practice on filing

When the deed has been executed it must be presented with:
- (a) the necessary statutory declaration;
- (b) the certificates, passport and immigration documents if relevant; and
- (c) any necessary consents and affidavits

to the Filing and Record Department of the Supreme Court for enrolment. Birth, marriage and other relevant certificates should be exhibited to the declaration, photocopies being acceptable in ordinary cases. *See also* reg 8 *below* where the application relates to enrolment of change of name of a child.

A draft of the *London Gazette* advertisement (*see below*) must be lodged at the same time. The new and former names that appear on the draft advertisement should be legibly written and not in the form of a signature. The advertisement itself is not required to be signed but it must, in all cases, bear the name and address of the maker of the deed or his solicitor.

A witness is not now required but, if there are any, the names and addresses of the witness or witnesses to the deed should be legibly written in block letters below their signatures. On acceptance of the document for enrolment, a *praecipe* is issued and the fees stated must be paid and the *praecipe* returned to the Department.

After enrolment the deed, endorsed with a certificate of enrolment, will be issued by post to the person or firm named in the advertisement. A copy of the *London Gazette* containing the advertisement will also subsequently be sent by the HMSO Publication Centre direct to the address on the advertisement.

Searches and copies

Enrolled copies of deeds poll are kept, and may be inspected, at the Filing Department, or at the Public Record Office, Chancery Lane, London WC2A 1LR according to the date of enrolment. Enrolment books more then five years old are periodically transferred from the Filing Department to the Record Office.

The search fee for the index of deeds still at the Central Office is £1 if the search is conducted in person, or £5 if the court conducts the search in response to a postal application. Copies may be obtained by parties, their solicitors, or by other persons on reasons being shown. Copies sealed by the Central Office are receivable in evidence under RSC Ord 38, r 10. The fees taken for copies which are photocopied from the manuscript or typescript of the original roll are 25p per page if size A4, foolscap or smaller; 40p per page if larger. It is not possible for a solicitor to produce his own copy of the original deed for examining with the enrolled copy and marking, because the solicitor's copy would differ from the enrolled copy which is retyped by the Central Office. It is advisable to enquire at the Central Office as to current fees.

Advertisement

Upon enrolment the deed poll must be advertised in the *London Gazette* by the clerk in charge for the time being of the Filing and Record Department at the Central Office of the Supreme Court: the 1994 Regulations, reg 7.

The expense of the advertisement required by reg 7 is borne by the applicant. The current fees applicable will be supplied on request by the Central Office.

Evidencing change of name of a child

Except as set out *below*, the 1994 Regulations apply in relation to a deed poll evidencing the change of name of a child as if the child were the applicant: the 1994 Regulations, reg 8 (1).

'Parental responsibility' has the meaning given in the Children Act 1989, s 3: the 1994 Regulations, reg 8(8). *See* Chapter 5.

Regulation 8(3)–(8), as set out *below*, does not apply to a married, female child who has attained the age of 16 (who must comply with the full Regulations) but does apply to any other child.

If the child is under 16, the deed poll must be executed by a person having parental responsibility for him: the 1994 Regulations, reg 8(3). If the child has attained the age of 16, the deed poll must not only be executed by a person having parental responsibility for him but the child must also endorse his consent by signing the same in both his old and his new names. The child's signature must be witnessed: the 1994 Regulations, reg 8(4).

There must be supplied with the application to enrol the deed:

(a) an affidavit that shows both that the change of name is for the benefit of the child, and that:

   (i) the application is submitted by all persons having parental responsibility for him; or

   (ii) the application is submitted by one person having parental responsibility for the child with the consent of every other such person; or

   (iii) the application is submitted by one person having parental responsibility for the child without the consent of every other such person, or by some other person whose name and capacity are given, for the reasons set out in the affidavit;

(b) in each individual case, whatever other evidence the Master of the Rolls may require: the 1994 Regulations, reg 8(5). *See below* as to *Practice Direction.*

The deed poll and documentary evidence of citizenship, etc mentioned in the 1994 Regulations, reg 3, must be exhibited to a statutory declaration by a Commonwealth citizen on the terms mentioned in the 1994 Regulations, reg 4(1), except that the declaration must state how long the householder has known both the person making the affidavit and the child respectively: the 1994 Regulations, reg 8(5)(*a*), (6).

A child under 16 is not required to sign a deed poll of change of name: the 1994 Regulations, reg 8(7).

Practice Direction (Child: Change of Surname) ('Practice Direction') (1995) *The Times,* 17 February (*see* Appendix B), revokes *Practice Direction (QBD) (Minors: Change of Surname)* [1977] 1 WLR 1065. The *Practice Direction,* art 1(*a*) states that where anyone who has acquired parental responsibility for a child by virtue of an order of the High Court, county court or family proceedings court, and has applied for the enrolment of a deed poll recording the change of surname of the child, then the applicant must, if the child is under 18 (unless she is female and married), supply with the application the written consent of every other person having parental responsibility.

If the consents required are not forthcoming the application to enrol will be adjourned generally, unless and until leave is given to change the child's surname in the proceedings in which the order was made, and the leave produced to the Filing Department: *Practice Direction,* art 1(*b*).

Where an application to enrol a deed poll evidencing the change of a child's name (if the child is under 18, unless female and married) is made by a person who has not been given parental responsibility as *above*, leave of the court to enrol the deed will be granted if the written consent of every person having parental responsibility is produced. If any person whose consent is required is dead or overseas, or if it is not possible to find such a person despite the exercise of reasonable diligence, the court will grant leave to enrol the deed: *Practice Direction*, art 2(*a*).

The Senior Master or the Practice Master will refer to the Master of the Rolls in doubtful cases, and where none of the conditions is complied with the matter might be referred to the Official Solicitor for investigation and report: *Practice Direction*, art 2(*b*) and (*c*).

Family deeds

The requirements as to citizenship, marital status and the special provisions relating to children should be complied with when a family deed is presented for enrolment.

Until 31 December 1948 a woman marrying a British subject became herself British in English law. This is no longer the case. If the applicant is a person naturalised before 1949, the certificate of naturalisation may include the wife and children. For naturalisation after 1948 this will not be so, and separate evidence of the citizenship of the wife and children will be needed.

If the application is for enrolment of a deed by a divorced person extending also to his or her children of the former marriage the written consent of the former spouse (being the parent of the children in question) must be filed or dispensed with by leave. If it is a dispensation case an affidavit evidencing that the change is in the best interests of the children must be lodged. If the divorced person has remarried the written consent of the step-parent should be exhibited to the affidavit, as a matter of good practice.

There have been a few cases in which several adult brothers and sisters have joined in one deed whereby they have all assumed a new or additional name, usually to satisfy an inheritance condition. In such a case the full new names and former names with addresses of all persons intended to be affected should be included. *See also* Chapter 4, and the requirements as laid down in the recent *Practice Direction above*.

Aliens

An alien, defined in British Nationality Act 1981, s 50 as a person who is neither a Commonwealth citizen, nor a British citizen, nor a citizen of the Republic of Ireland, may change his name and evidence that change by deed poll as well as, for example, by informal assumption. The change will be as effective in English law as one made by a Commonwealth citizen. However, a deed poll by an alien will not be accepted for enrolment as the applicant will not be able to satisfy of the 1994 Regulations, reg 2(1)–(3).

Forenames and Christian names

Deeds purporting to effect a change of forename or Christian name are accepted for enrolment. *See further* Chapter 2 as to the law relating to change of forenames and Christian names.

As regards Christian names a certificate must be filed to the effect that: 'Notwithstanding the decision of Mr Justice Vaisey in *Re Parrott, Cox v Parrott*, the applicant desires the enrolment to proceed'. The applicant thus takes the risk of the deed subsequently being declared ineffective so far as the change of Christian name is concerned. The Filing Department prefers the certificate to be endorsed on the deed itself, rather than the householder's declaration, so that it becomes part of the enrolled deed.

Citizenship

Commonwealth citizenship

A Commonwealth citizen is one who is either:
- (a) a British citizen, a British Dependent Territories citizen, a British Overseas citizen, a British National (Overseas) or a British subject; or
- (b) a citizen of a country specified in the British Nationality Act 1981, Sched 3 by virtue of a law for the time being in force in that country: British Nationality Act 1981, s 37(1).

At the date of commencement of the 1981 Act, Sched 3 named all the countries belonging to the Commonwealth which had become independent. As more countries become independent, they are normally added to the Schedule by statutory amendment. Part 1 of Appendix C lists the countries within Sched 3.

British citizenship

British citizenship is the main category of British nationality and the only one which carries the right to reside in the United Kingdom. Automatic acquisition as at 1 January 1983, the commencement date of the British

Nationality Act 1981, includes deemed acquisition under the British Nationality (Falklands Islands) Act 1983, as amended. *See below* at p 101.

British citizenship may be acquired under the British Nationality Act 1981, Pt I, ss 1–14 as follows:

Section 1   Birth or adoption

If a person is born in the United Kingdom on or after 1 January 1983 he will be a British citizen if, at the time of the birth, his father or mother is either:

(a) a British citizen; or

(b) settled in the United Kingdom.

'Settled', for these purposes, means ordinarily resident in the United Kingdom, without being subject to any provision of the immigration laws restricting the period for which a person may remain: British Nationality Act 1981, s 50(2). *See also* s 50(3)–(4) which provides that a person is not regarded as settled if he is entitled to certain exemptions under the Immigration Act 1971. (However, the father or mother is considered settled if they were settled in the United Kingdom immediately before becoming entitled to such an exemption, and they were ordinarily resident in the United Kingdom from becoming entitled to the exemption up until the birth.)

'Ordinarily resident' is not defined in the British Nationality Act 1981. A person is not ordinarily resident in the United Kingdom at any time when in breach of its immigration laws.

There are special provisions for those born on ships or aircraft outside the United Kingdom: *see* the British Nationality Act 1981, s 50(7).

A new-born infant found abandoned in the United Kingdom is (unless the contrary be shown) deemed to have been born in the United Kingdom to a parent who satisfies the conditions laid down in the British Nationality Act 1981, s 1(1): British Nationality Act 1981, s 1(2).

A person may acquire British citizenship by registration: British Nationality Act 1981, s 1(3) and (4). *See below* at p 99.

If a minor who is not a British citizen is adopted pursuant to a United Kingdom court order, then he acquires British citizenship as from the date of the order if on that date the adopter (or in the case of a joint adoption, one of the adopters) is himself a British citizen: British Nationality Act 1981, s 1(5).

Section 2   Acquisition by descent

If a person is born outside the United Kingdom on or after 1 January 1983 then he will be a British citizen if at the time of the birth his father or mother is:

(a) a British citizen otherwise than by descent; or

(b) a British citizen serving outside the United Kingdom in, eg Crown service under the United Kingdom government, recruitment for that service having taken place in the United Kingdom; or

(c) a British citizen serving outside the United Kingdom in a European Community institution, recruitment for that service having taken place in a country which at the time of the recruitment was a member of the Communities (these being the European Economic Community, the European Coal and Steel Community and the European Atomic Energy Community) (*see* the European Communities Act 1972, s 1(2)).

For further reading as to Community institutions *see* the European Communities Act 1972, Sched 1, Pt II. *See also* the British Nationality Act 1981, s 14 for the meaning of British citizen by descent, and *Halsbury's Laws of England* 4th edn (Butterworth & Co). *See also* the British Citizenship (Designated Service) Order 1982 (SI No 1004), as amended.

Section 3   Acquisition by registration—minors
A minor may be registered as a British citizen, on application to the Secretary of State.

Section 4   Acquisition by registration
British Dependent Territories citizens, British Nationals (Overseas), British Overseas citizens, British subjects under the British Nationality Act 1981 or British protected persons (*see below* at pp 103–105 for definitions) are *entitled* by virtue of residence, on application, to be registered as British citizens, if they satisfy certain conditions.

Section 5   Acquisition by registration—nationals for the purpose of the Community Treaties
British Dependent Territories citizens treated as nationals of the United Kingdom for the purposes of the Community Treaties are *entitled*, on application, to be registered as British citizens.

Sections 41 and 42 of the British Nationality Act 1981 deal with Regulations and Orders in Council relating to registration and naturalisation.

Section 6   Acquisition by naturalisation
If the Secretary of State thinks fit and is satisfied that the requirements of the British Nationality Act 1981, Sched 1 are satisfied, he may, on application, grant a certificate of naturalisation to:

(a) a person of full age and capacity; or

(b) one who on the date of the application is married to a British citizen.

Section 7   Registration by virtue of residence in the United Kingdom or relevant employment
There is a *right* to registration as a British citizen, by virtue of residence, in certain circumstances, on application made within five, six or eight years after 1 January 1983, and on satisfying certain requirements.

Section 8   Registration by virtue of marriage
A woman has a *right* to registration as a British citizen on marriage if, immediately before 1 January 1983 (and on application made within five years of 1 January 1983), she was the wife of a citizen of the United Kingdom and Colonies and on satisfying certain conditions.

Section 9   Registration by virtue of father's citizenship
A person born in a foreign country has a *right*, on application (made within five years of 1 January 1983 and within 12 months of birth) to registration as a British citizen by virtue of his father's British citizenship, and on satisfying certain conditions.

Section 10   Registration following renunciation of citizenship of the United Kingdom and Colonies
If a person would have been entitled to be registered as a citizen of the United Kingdom and Colonies in certain conditions under the British Nationality Act 1964, before 1 January 1983, he is entitled on application to be registered as a British citizen.

Section 11   Citizens of the United Kingdom and Colonies who became British citizens on 1 January 1983
A person who, as at 31 December 1982, was a citizen of the United Kingdom and Colonies and had the right to reside in the United Kingdom under the Immigration Act 1971 (as in force on 31 December 1982), *acquired* British citizenship as from 1 January 1983.

Section 12   Renunciation of British citizenship
A British citizen (having attained the age of 18, or married under that age, and of full capacity) who makes a declaration of renunciation of British citizenship in prescribed manner, ceases to be a British citizen on registration of the document. *See also* the British Nationality Act 1981, s 41 as to any regulations made for registration.

Section 12(1) applies to a British National (Overseas) (*see below*) as it applies to British citizens and British Overseas citizens (*see below*): *see* the Hong Kong (British Nationality) Order 1986 (SI No 948), art 7(10).

Section 13   Resumption of British citizenship

A person who has ceased to be a British citizen as a result of a declaration of renunciation is *entitled* to be registered as a British citizen if he is of full capacity and his prior renunciation of British citizenship was necessary to enable him to retain or acquire some other citizenship or nationality. A person is only entitled to registration under this section on one occasion.

Section 40   Deprivation of British citizenship

The Secretary of State has a discretion to deprive a person of their British citizenship which they have acquired by registration or naturalisation, if it was obtained by fraud, false representation or concealment of any material fact: *see* the British Nationality Act 1981, s 40. Registration or naturalisation will be deemed to have been of no effect if originally obtained by serious fraud, and of course a person cannot be deprived of citizenship which he never acquired.

There are also provisions whereby a person may be deprived of citizenship on the grounds of disloyalty or imprisonment: *see* the British Nationality Act 1981, s 40(3) and (4).

Special cases

The Falklands—Deemed acquisition of British citizenship   The British Nationality (Falklands Islands) Act 1983 is deemed to have been in force as at 1 January 1983. The people of the Colony of the Falkland Islands and Dependencies (a British Dependent Territory) automatically and retrospectively acquired British citizenship as from 1 January 1983, and by birth or adoption after that: *see* the British Nationality (Falklands Islands) Act 1983, s 5(2).

Certain applicants may be registered at the discretion of the Secretary of State: *see* the British Nationality (Falkland Islands) Act 1983, s 2(1), as amended by the Hong Kong (British Nationality) Order 1986 (SI No 948) and the British Nationality (Falkland Islands) Act 1983, s 2(2), similarly amended.

Hong Kong—acquisition of British citizenship by registration   See also *below* at p 106 for British Nationals (Overseas).

Hong Kong will cease to be a dependent territory on 1 July 1997, and it is removed from the list of dependent territories set out in the British Nationality Act 1981, Sched 6 with effect from 1 July 1997. *See* generally the Hong Kong (British Nationality) Order 1986 (SI No 948), as amended; and the British Nationality (Hong Kong) Regulations 1986 (SI No 2175) which carry the effect of the provisions of SI No 948, as amended. *See also* the British Nationality (Hong Kong) Registration of Citizens) Regulations 1990 (SI No 2211), the British Nationality (Hong Kong) (Selection Scheme) Order 1990 (SI No 2292), as amended and the British Nationality (Hong Kong) Act 1990.

Under the British Nationality (Hong Kong) Act 1990, which came into force on 7 November 1990 (save for s 2(2)), there is special provision whereby the Secretary of State must, before 30 June 1997, register up to 50,000 persons of good character as British citizens. These persons will have been recommended to him for that purpose by the Governor of Hong Kong under a scheme or schemes made by Order in Council. The applicants must be settled in Hong Kong and be:

(a) British Dependent Territories citizens by virtue of a connection with Hong Kong; or

(b) British Nationals (Overseas); or

(c) British Overseas citizens; or

(d) British subjects; or

(e) British protected persons; or

(f) persons who applied before 26 July 1990 for registration or naturalisation as British Dependent Territories citizens by virtue of a connection with Hong Kong provided that, in the absence of registration as British citizens, that application would have been successful.

Connection   For the definition of 'connection' *see* the British Nationality (Hong Kong) Act 1990, s 1(1) and Sched 1, para 4(3) applying the Hong Kong (British Nationality) Order 1986 (SI No 948), art 2.

Those registered under the British Nationality (Hong Kong) Act 1990, s 1(1) and Sched 2 will be British citizens other than by descent, and British citizens by descent respectively: British Nationality (Hong Kong) Act 1990, s 2(1).

The Secretary of State must register as a British citizen:

(a) the spouse of a person registered under the British Nationality (Hong Kong) Act 1990, s 1(1); and

(b) any minor child of such a person,

if the spouse or the child is recommended to the Secretary of State for that purpose by the Governor of Hong Kong. *See further* the British Nationality (Hong Kong) Act 1990, Scheds 1 and 2.

An illegitimate child is, for these purposes, the mother's child and not the father's. As to the position of legitimated and posthumous children in Hong Kong *see* the British Nationality Act 1981, ss 47, 48 and 50(9) as applied by the British Nationality (Hong Kong) Act 1990, s 2(3).

British Dependent Territories citizenship

Since 1 January 1983, a British Dependent Territories citizen is one who (if at the time of his birth his father or mother is a British Dependent Territories citizen or is settled in a dependent territory) falls within one of ss 15–25 of the British Nationality Act 1981 by reason of birth in, or a connection with, one of the countries named in Sched 6 to the Act (loosely called 'colonies').

See above at p 101 for separate provisions conferring British citizenship on Falkland Islanders.

As countries attain independent status, or are included in newly-independent states, their names are removed from Sched 6. The present composition of Sched 6 is as set out in Appendix C at p 141. Hong Kong will cease to be a British Dependent Territory on 1 July 1997.

Citizenship is acquired under the sections of the British Nationality Act 1981 as follows:

- s 15—acquisition by birth or adoption;
- s 16—acquisition by descent;
- s 17—acquisition by registration (minors);
- s 18—acquisition by naturalisation;
- s 19—right to registration by virtue of residence in a dependent territory;
- s 20—registration by virtue of marriage;
- s 21—right to registration by virtue of father's citizenship;
- s 22—right to registration replacing the right to resume citizenship of the United Kingdom and Colonies;
- s 23—citizens of the United Kingdom and Colonies who became British Dependent Territories citizens at commencement;
- s 24—renunciation and resumption;
- s 25—meaning of British Dependent Territories citizen by descent.

As to some British Dependent Territories citizens with Falkland Islands connections having become British citizens, *see* the British Nationality (Falklands Islands) Act 1983, and *above* at p 101.

British Overseas citizenship

As from 1 January 1983 the law relating to British Overseas citizenship is contained in the British Nationality Act 1981, Pt III. Briefly, any person who was a citizen of the United Kingdom and Colonies on 31 December 1982, and who did not become either a British citizen or a British Dependent Territories citizen on 1 January 1983, became a British Overseas citizen. There is no right to reside in the United Kingdom: British Nationality Act 1981, s 26.

This category provided British citizenship for those persons who would otherwise have lost it when citizenship of the United Kingdom and Colonies became defunct on 1 January 1983. A person cannot become a British Overseas citizen by birth, descent, or by naturalisation, and the citizenship will disappear in the course of time. It can, in limited circumstances, be used to give status to a person who might otherwise be stateless.

When Hong Kong ceases to be a dependent territory (*see above* at p 102, and China resumes sovereignty, those who have British Dependent Territories citizenship by virtue (wholly or partly) of a connection with Hong Kong will lose it. There will be those who acquire British citizenship by virtue of the special scheme (*see above* at pp 101–102) or become British Nationals (Overseas) (*see below* at p 106), but not all Hong Kong residents will acquire either status. They and their subsequently-born children and grandchildren could become stateless.

It is provided by the Hong Kong Act 1985, para 2(1)*(a),* Sched 3 and the Hong Kong (British Nationality) Order 1986 (SI No 948), arts 3, 6(1) that a person who loses British Dependent Territories citizenship on 1 July 1997 because he held it by virtue of a connection with Hong Kong and who would otherwise become stateless, will become a British Overseas citizen on that date.

A person will be a British Overseas citizen by birth if he is born, otherwise stateless, on or after 1 July 1997 if at the time of his birth either:

  (a) one of his parents is a British National (Overseas): *see below* at p 106, or

  (b) one of his parents is a British Overseas citizen who automatically became such on 1 July 1997: *see* the Hong Kong Act 1985, para 2(3), and the Hong Kong (British Nationality) Order 1986 (SI No 948), art 6(2).

A child of a male or female British Overseas citizen (who acquired citizenship by birth under art 6(2) *above* and who was still a British Overseas citizen at the time of their child's birth) born outside the dependent territories on or after 1 July 1997, is *entitled* to be registered as a British Overseas citizen if:

(a) he was born stateless; and

(b) an application is made within 12 months of the birth (or in certain circumstances six years at the discretion of the Secretary of State): Hong Kong (British Nationality) Order 1986 (SI No 948), art 6(5); and

(c) the father or mother of that parent was on 30 June 1997 a British Dependent Territories citizen otherwise than by descent by virtue of having a connection with Hong Kong, or would have been but for his or her death: Hong Kong (British Nationality) Order 1986 (SI No 948), art 6(3), (4).

Renunciation of British Overseas citizenship can be effected by declaration provided the person has or acquires within six months some other citizenship or nationality: British Nationality Act 1981, s 29. However, the status cannot be resumed.

Sections 27–28 of the British Nationality Act 1981 provide for registration of minors and registration by virtue of marriage.

British subjects

The provisions contained in the British Nationality Act 1981, ss 30–35 provide for the continuation of British subject status for those who were British subjects without citizenship prior to the commencement of the British Nationality Act 1981.

A person who, on 31 December 1982, was either:

(a) a British subject without citizenship by virtue of the British Nationality Act 1948, ss 13–16; or

(b) a British subject by virtue of the British Nationality Act 1965 (which deals with the registration, as British subjects, of alien women who have been married to certain British subjects),

acquired British subject status by virtue of the British Nationality Act 1981, s 30.

Section 31 of the British Nationality Act 1981 deals with the continuance as British subjects of some former citizens of Eire who were also British subjects before 1949. Section 32 of the British Nationality Act 1981 deals with registration of minors (at the discretion of the Secretary of State) and the registration of some alien women entitled to registration as British subjects on 31 December 1982. Sections 34–35 deal with renunciation (as for British Overseas citizens) and the circumstances in which the status can be lost, eg acquisition of any other nationality.

British Nationals (Overseas)

The British Nationality (Hong Kong) Act 1990 provides for selected Hong Kong residents, their spouses and minor children, to acquire British citizenship. The status, which does not carry the right to reside in the United Kingdom, provides British nationality for the people of Hong Kong *before* they lose their British Dependent Territories citizenship. *See above* at p 104.

Any person who is a British Dependent Territories citizen by virtue (wholly or partly) of a connection with Hong Kong and who, but for that connection with Hong Kong would *not* be a British Dependent Territories citizen, is *entitled,* before 1 July 1997, to be registered as a British National (Overseas) and to hold or be included in a passport appropriate to that status: *see* the Hong Kong (British Nationality) Order 1986 (SI No 948), art 4(2), and its definition of 'connection' for these purposes. *See also* the application of the definition by the British Nationality (Hong Kong) Act 1990, s 1(1) and Sched 1, para 4(3).

Those born between 1 January 1997 and 30 June 1997 can acquire the status up until the end of 1997: Hong Kong (British Nationality) Order 1986 (SI No 948), art 4(2).

If a person registered as a British National (Overseas) ceases to be a British Dependent Territories citizen before 1 July 1997, he will automatically lose his British National (Overseas) status: Hong Kong (British Nationality) Order 1986 (SI No 948), art 4(3). However, automatic loss of British Dependent Territories citizenship on 1 July 1997 will not lead to loss of British National (Overseas) status: *see* the Hong Kong (British Nationality) Order 1986 (SI No 948), art 3.

The status can be renounced by declaration provided that the person has, or acquires within six months, some other citizenship or nationality: *see* the Hong Kong (British Nationality) Order 1986 (SI No 948), art 7 (applying the British Nationality Act 1981, s 12—*see above* at pp 100–101). However, the status cannot be resumed.

Again, as for British citizens, persons may be deprived of British subjecthood on the ground of fraud, false representation or concealment of material fact, disloyalty or imprisonment: *see* the Hong Kong (British Nationality) Order 1986 (SI No 948) art 7, applying the British Nationality Act 1981, s 40.

Registration will be deemed of no effect if it were obtained by serious and causative fraud.

Chapter 8

Other Methods of Evidencing a Change of Name

Operation of law

Marriage confers a name upon a woman which becomes her actual name and remains so even after divorce or bereavement: *see Fendall v Goldsmid* (1877) 2 PD 263; *Cowley v Cowley* [1901] AC 450 and Chapter 2. Although it is generally the custom for a married woman to be known by her husband's surname, it is quite open to her to retain her maiden name if she wishes, and many women now do so. In *Re Fry* [1945] Ch 348 Vaisey J said: 'There is, so far as I know, nothing to compel a married woman to use her husband's surname'.

Letters of administration to the estate of a deceased woman who has been divorced have long been granted in the name by which she has passed and was known at the time of her death, which is usually the married name: *see In the Goods of Augusta Hay* (1865) LR 1 P & D 51.

Similarly, on succession to or grant of a peerage or dignity the law may operate to change a person's former name: *see Lapiere v Sir John Germain Knight and Baronet & the Duchess of Norfolk* (1703) 2 Ld Raym 859 where it was held that a title or dignity is part of the name of the person who holds the title and he should be described by his full title even in a court action. Sir John was sued only by the title of Baronet and successfully pleaded in abatement that he should have been sued as Knight and Baronet.

There are instances where peers have continued to be known by their original names. A disclaimer under the Peerage Act 1963 will naturally also effect a change of name.

In practice there may less often be a surname change on succession to a baronetcy. When the Lucas-Tooth baronetcy was recreated in 1920, Mr Hugh Warrand took his new name by Royal Licence: (1985) *The Times*, 20 November.

Notarial instrument

Evidence of a change of name may be provided by a notarial act combined with a declaration, and this method may be found particularly appropriate where evidence is required in a form which will carry weight internationally, for example if the individual proposes to emigrate. The expense may be somewhat greater than that of an unenrolled deed poll unsupported by a notarial act.

A notary public will prepare a statutory declaration whereby the declarant, after giving particulars of his citizenship and its derivation, renounces a former surname and assumes a new one. A change in a non-baptismal forename, or an addition to it, may be incorporated if required.

The declaration is then made before the notary, who authenticates it as a notarial act and enters it on his register. Certainly in the case of a Commonwealth citizen such an instrument will be found generally acceptable here and in many places abroad, particularly in the common law countries.

See further Delafield's *The Provincial Notary*, which also indicates the possibility of a family instrument, all the participants being adult.

Statutory declaration

A change of name may be evidenced by statutory declaration made before a Justice of the Peace, notary public, Commissioner for Oaths, practising solicitor (not acting or interested in the matter: Solicitors Act 1974, s 81), or other officer authorised by law to administer an oath.

The declaration, which must be in the form prescribed by the Schedule to the Statutory Declarations Act 1835, should set out that the declarant desires to change his name, and intends henceforth to be known by the name of X and renounces his former name of Y. A similar declaration can be made, *mutatis mutandis*, by any person having parental responsibility on behalf of a child. *See* Appendix D for current fees.

A statutory declaration cannot be enrolled in the Supreme Court. Further weight of evidence may be attached by advertising the declaration in the local and/or national press (*see below*).

Advertisement in the press

Such advertisement may be the only form of written evidence of a change of name, and clearly copies should be carefully preserved.

Advertisement may accompany a change of name by statutory declaration (*see above*) and deeds poll enrolled in the Supreme Court and changes of name by Royal Licence will be advertised in the *London Gazette*.

It is stated in Public Record Office Information Sheet No 38 (Change of Name) that between 1939 and 1945 a British subject could only change his name if he had published a notice giving details of the proposed change in the *London, Edinburgh* or *Belfast Gazette*, 21 days before assuming the new name.

College of Arms

A change of name may be evidenced by deed poll prepared and recorded at the College of Arms, Queen Victoria Street, London EC4V 4BT. The person whose name is changed need not be a person bearing arms. The change is notified in the *London Gazette*. There is no standard fee, each application being dealt with according to its own facts, but it is likely, at the time of writing, to be in the region of £250.

The College will also record a deed which has been prepared elsewhere, whether or not it has been enrolled in the Central Office of the Supreme Court.

The records of the College are not open to public inspection, but the officers of the College will cause them to be searched, and certified extracts to be supplied in appropriate cases.

The College will not, however, enrol a deed poll purporting to change a person's Christian name.

Royal Licence

There is mention in *Halsbury's Laws of England* 4th edn (Butterworth & Co), vol 35 at para 1278 n1 of what is thought to be the first grant of a Royal Licence for a change of name: in 1679 the name of Percie was assumed by the Earl of Ogle, son of the Duke of Newcastle.

This method, which is sometimes stipulated in name and arms clauses in wills or settlements (*see generally* Chapter 4), involves an application, with reasons, through the College of Arms for the grant of a licence under the Royal Sign Manual. The procedure and criteria generally applied are described in *Halsbury's* (as *above*) at para 974 et seq. Briefly, a person should apply to the College of Arms for a petition to be drawn up by one of the Officers of Arms. It is then signed by the applicant and submitted to the Sovereign through the Home Secretary. The Sovereign is advised by the Home Secretary and has a discretion as to the granting of the licence. The writer understands that no precise rules are specified for the exercise of the discretion, but it is stated in *Halsbury's* that if the request for the grant is made so as to comply with a name and arms clause in a will or settlement, especially if linked with a defeasance clause, then it is normally granted. However, if there are no reasonable grounds for the application then it is likely to be rejected.

Fees are payable to the College of Arms and the Home Office for the Royal Licence for the change of name and arms. In addition, a further sum is payable for the grant or exemplification of arms under the said licence and to meet the cost of publishing the terms of the licence in the *London Gazette*.

It is suggested that an enquiry be made of the College of Arms as to current procedure requirements and fees prior to pursuing this method of obtaining documentary evidence of a desired change of name.

Act of Parliament

This method, which is costly and requires the promotion of a private personal Bill, is rarely resorted to. *See* the Clifton's Name Act 1859 and the Baines Name Act 1907 (the latter being the last instance of a change of name by this method). *See Halsbury's Laws of England* (as *above*), vol 34 for the procedure for the presentation of a petition for a Bill. The House of Lords' Record Office holds the original Acts of Parliament, if inspection is required, where the private Acts of change of name are not recorded in the officially printed series of Acts, together with other papers leading to the promotion of such private Bills.

Public Record Office

The facilities available at this Office afford a means whereby access may be obtained to records of changes of name by deed or by Royal Licence as outlined *above*.

The following may be seen at the Public Record Office, Chancery Lane, London WC2A 1LR:

(1) Enrolment books, after removal from the Filing Department of the Central Office of the Supreme Court. Such books less than three years old may be searched in Room 81, Royal Courts of Justice, Strand, London WC2A 2LL.

(2) The Close Rolls of Chancery (up until 1903) on which earlier deeds are enrolled.

(3) State papers relating to change of name by Royal Licence.

Home Office Records relating to change of name by Royal Licence may be seen at the Public Record Office at Ruskin Avenue, Kew, Richmond, Surrey.

The Public Record Office produces General Information Leaflet No 19 on obtaining reprographic copies of records, and Form 10—Ordering documents at Chancery Lane by Computer.

The fee for certification is £4 per document and it is advisable to enquire as to any increase.

There are agencies which make searches on a commercial footing. The Public Record Office will search for an enrolment for a period of five years from a given date and, if successful, will provide an estimate of the cost of certified or uncertified photocopies.

Scotland

Changes of name in Scotland may be recorded in the Registers of the Court of the Lord Lyon which are held at HM House, Edinburgh 2.

Chapter 9

Solicitors—Change of Name on the Roll

The roll maintained by the Law Society under the Solicitors Act 1974, s 6, normally describes a solicitor by the name he or she bore at the time of admission as a solicitor. Whether the solicitor practises or not, the name on the roll can only be changed in accordance with regulations made by the Master of the Rolls (with the concurrence of the Lord Chancellor and the Lord Chief Justice) under the Solicitors Act 1974, s 28 (as amended by the Administration of Justice Act 1985, s 8 and Sched 1, para 8).

The regulations which came into effect on 1 February 1989 are the Solicitors (Keeping of the Roll) Regulations 1989, as amended by the Solicitors (Keeping of the Rolls) (Amendment) Regulations 1991 (together 'the 1989 Regulations'). Regulations 12–15 in Pts IV and V are applicable to an application for a change of name by a solicitor.

Regulation 12(*a*) and (*b*) provides that the Society may, in two specific cases, make the appropriate change to the roll simply on production to the Society of satisfactory evidence of the change. These cases are:

    (a) a change of a female solicitor's name in consequence of marriage; and

    (b) the acquisition of a title.

It appears from the wording of Form KR5 set out in the Schedule to the 1989 Regulations that it would be appropriate to use this form of application in these cases, if desired. However, it has been the practice of the Records Department to accept a letter supported by documentary evidence of the acquisition of the new name.

In cases other than mentioned *above* a formal application to the Society by the solicitor on Form KR5 (or in a form to like effect) is necessary, this being supported by a deed poll or a statutory declaration by the applicant providing satisfactory evidence of the change of name. It does not appear that an enrolled deed poll is necessary: the 1989 Regulations, reg 13.

Form KR5 calls for a statement of the existing name as shown on the roll and the new name the solicitor desires to be recorded. The following details must also be supplied:

(a) the style under which the applicant is practising at the time of the application and under which he intends to practise after the change;

(b) the date of admission;

(c) all past, present and proposed places of business; and

(d) present private addresses.

The supporting evidence must be specified in the application, and must either accompany the application or be produced to the Society before the change of name on the roll can be effected.

Upon receipt, the Society must display the application in the Society's Hall, and otherwise publicise, as it thinks fit, certain of the particulars given in the application: the 1989 Regulations, reg 14(*a*). In addition, in case there is a risk the solicitor might be confused with any other solicitor or firm of solicitors, the Society must notify those same particulars to such solicitor or firm: the 1989 Regulations, reg 14(*b*).

As well as surnames, Christian names and forenames appearing on the roll may be the subject of change.

If the application is granted the Society causes the name on the roll to be amended. In practice an announcement of the Society's grant of the application normally appears in the Law Society *Gazette*.

Any person who wishes to appeal against the Society's refusal to grant his application for change of his name on the roll may do so within 28 days of the notice of the Society's decision.

Appeals are to be made to the Master of the Rolls under the Master of the Rolls (Appeals and Applications) Regulations 1991, as amended by the Master of the Rolls (Appeals and Applications) (Amendment) Regulations) 1994 (together 'the 1991 Regulations'): the 1989 Regulations, reg 15 and *see* the 1991 Regulations, reg 3, para (xix).

These Regulations, which came into force on 1 February 1991, supersede the 1964, 1966 and 1975 Regulations relating to appeals and applications: the 1991 Regulations, reg 1. They provide for a petition signed by the applicant, stating the circumstances and the matters of fact relied on in support of his appeal to be lodged with the Clerk to the Master of the Rolls. At the same time there must be lodged a statutory declaration confirming the facts and exhibiting any necessary documents. Within two days of lodging the petition and supporting documents, copies of the same must be lodged with the Society: the 1991 Regulations, reg 5.

Within six weeks of being supplied with the copy documents, the Society has the right, if it so wishes, to make written submissions on the substance of the appeal, or the Master of the Rolls's jurisdiction in the matter. Copies of those written submissions must be sent to the applicant: the 1991 Regulations, reg 5A.

The Master of the Rolls appoints a time for hearing the appeal. Normally six weeks are allowed from the date of the petition, but an earlier date may be appointed on request in proper cases: the 1991 Regulations, reg 6.

At the hearing the appellant solicitor and the Society may appear in person; either side may be heard through solicitor or counsel, and the strict rules of evidence will not apply: the 1991 Regulations, regs 7 and 8.

The Master of the Rolls may make such order as to costs as he thinks fit, his discretion being unfettered by anything in the Regulations: the 1991 Regulations, reg 8A.

The Master of the Rolls may make such order as he shall think fit in relation to the appeal, signing the same. His Secretary then files the order with the Society which must take the action required to give effect to the order: the 1991 Regulations, reg 9.

Appendix A

Forms

Form 1: Deed poll on change of name

('A')

THIS CHANGE OF NAME DEED (intended to be enrolled at the Central Office)[1] made this   day of   19

By me the undersigned[2]

of[3]

now or lately called[4]

a [British citizen/British Dependent Territories citizen/British Overseas citizen] [Commonwealth citizen] under section   of the British Nationality Act 1981[5]

WITNESSES AND IT IS HEREBY DECLARED [on behalf of myself and my wife and my children][6] as follows:

1   I absolutely and entirely renounce relinquish and abandon the use of my said former surname[7] of   and assume adopt and determine to take and use [from the date hereof][8] the surname[7] of   in substitution for my former surname[7] of

2   I shall at all times hereafter in all records deeds documents and other writings and in all actions and proceedings as well as in all dealings and transactions and on all occasions whatsoever use and subscribe the said name of   as my surname[7] in substitution for my former surname[7] of   so relinquished as aforesaid to the intent that I [my wife and my children][6] may hereafter be called known or distinguished not by the former surname[7] of   but by the surname[7] of   only.

3   I authorise and require all persons at all times to designate describe and address me [my wife and my children][6] by the adopted surname[7] of

IN WITNESS whereof I have hereunto subscribed my Christian or first name or names of   [9] and my adopted and substituted surname[7] of

                                                                            .

SIGNED AS A DEED AND DELIVERED
by the above-named   )
)   ....[9]
                              in   )
the presence of[10]   )
)   [formerly known as
)   ....]

---

[1]   Omit if made by an alien (see p 96) or not otherwise intended to be enrolled.

[2]   The new name in full.

[3]   If it is intended that the deed shall be enrolled, it must describe the applicant (whether man or woman) as single, married, widowed or divorced, as the case may be (see reg 2(4), p 91). In the case where the applicant is divorced it may be desirable to use the expression 'who has obtained a divorce from . . .' or 'who has been divorced by . . .'; and, if ordinary conveyancing practice is to be followed, a married woman should be described as 'the wife of . . .' In a case where the deed is intended to affect a child of a marriage which is void or has been annulled (see, eg Legitimacy Act 1976, s 1), it would seem right to record the void or avoided marriage as part of the applicant's description, thus, 'whose marriage to . . . was [void for . . .] or [annulled by a competent court on . . .].' In a case where there is no such child it does not seem necessary to mention a void or avoided marriage.

[4]   Or 'formerly called' if the change has already taken place. State, in any case, the full name relinquished.

[5]   Make the appropriate deletions: see reg 2, p 90. If the deed is not intended to be enrolled at the Central Office the reference to citizenship is unnecessary but preferable in case the deed is enrolled at a later date.

[6]   Delete such of the words in brackets as are inapplicable: as to the desirability of naming the wife and any existing children, and generally, see pp 94, 96. This may be done by adding the word 'namely' and setting out the full names of the wife and children. The words in square brackets are applicable only where the deed effects a change of surname. If a change of forename also is evidenced by the deed a variation of clause 3 will be appropriate making the new surname, but not the new forename, applicable to wife and children.

[7]   If it is desired to change a forename the word 'name' should be substituted for 'surname' and the old and new names should be set out in full, eg (former) 'John Frank Brown' (new) 'John Hugh Brown' (or 'John Hugh Smith' if both forename and surname are to be changed. See also the suggested wording at p 97.

[8]   Omit the words in square brackets if the change of name has already taken place.

[9]   The deed must be signed in both the old and the new names (reg 6, p 93). It is best to sign with the full Christian names, not initials.

[10] Signatures, names and addresses of witnesses (see p 89). It is not strictly necessary to have witnesses but is generally advisable to have two witnesses. Some professional bodies require it, as does the Central Office in the case of a child. When the deed is presented for enrolment, witnesses' names and addresses should be written in block letter under their signatures.

Form 2: Deed poll on change of name—shorter form not intended for enrolment

THIS CHANGE OF NAME DEED is made this   day
of   by me the undersigned formerly called

1   I declare that I have absolutely relinquished and abandoned the use of my
former names of   and in substitution therefor I have adopted
and hereby formally assume the names of

2   I intend at all times hereafter to use only the names   and
hereby authorise all persons to designate and address me accordingly.

SIGNED AS A DEED AND DELIVERED
    by the above named
                                    in
    the presence of

                                          ....

                                          formerly known as
                                          ....

See generally the notes to Form 1.

Form 3: Consent of spouse

(See p 91)

I,

of

the [husband] [wife] of [the within-named]

of

hereby certify that I have been given notice of the intention of the said

to apply for the enrolment of [the within-written Change of Name deed] [a deed evidencing [her] [his] change of name from   to   ] and I hereby consent [to the change of name of my said [wife] [husband] as therein witnessed] [to the said change of my [wife's] [husband's] name] and to the enrolment of the said deed in the Central Office of the Supreme Court of Judicature.

(Signed)

Witness

Notes

(1) The spouse's consent should, in ordinary cases, be endorsed on the deed. The regulations do not require the consent to be witnessed by a solicitor, but it seems desirable that it should be signed before a responsible and identifiable person, who should add his address and the position he holds.

(2) As to the consent of a child on an application to court a deed evidencing his or her change of name *see* pp 94–5.

Form 4: Simple form of consent of mother, or father with parental responsibility to change the name of a child

(To be endorsed on Family Deed executed either by father with parental responsibility, or mother) (*see* generally Chapter 5)

I

of

the [wife] [husband] of the within-named

and the [mother] [father] of [name and age of child/children]

being [a child] [children] of the said

and [a person] [persons] whose change of name is evidenced by the within-written deed hereby consent to the said change of name of the said [child] [children] as witnessed within and to the enrolment of the said deed in the Central Office of the Supreme Court.

(Signed)

Witness (*cf note (1) to Form 3*)

Notes

(1) This form may be used where children who have not yet attained the age of 16 are included in the Deed. Children of 16 and over must endorse their own consent (reg 8(4) of the 1994 Regulations). The form is appropriate where there are no persons with parental responsibility other than the mother and father.

Form 5: Consent of other person having parental responsibility

(To be endorsed on a deed of change of name of a child)

I

of

being a person with parental responsibility for [name and age of each child] whose change of name is evidenced by the within-written deed hereby consent to the said change of name of the said [name of each child] as witnessed within [and to the enrolment of the said deed in the Central Office of the Supreme Court]

(Signed)

Witness (*cf note (1) to Form 3*)

Notes

(1) This form may be used where, eg a change of a child's name is made where a residence order or care order is in force with respect to the child (CA 1989, ss 13(1), 33(7)), whether or not the deed is to be enrolled, and in cases covered by *Practice Direction* (1995) *The Times*, 17 February (*see* p 95).

Form 6: Deed poll by a person having parental responsibility on change of name of a child

THIS CHANGE OF NAME DEED (intended to be enrolled at the Central Office)[1] made this   of   19
By me [us][2] the undersigned

[a person] [the persons] having parental responsibility for[3]   of
                              (now or lately called[4]   )
(who is a child of the age of[5]   years single and a [British citizen]
[British Dependent Territories citizen] [British Overseas citizen]
[Commonwealth citizen] under section   of the British Nationality Act
1981])[6] on behalf of the said[3]

WITNESSES AND IT IS HEREBY DECLARED as follows:

1   On behalf of the said[3]   I [we] absolutely and entirely
renounce relinquish and abandon the use of his [her] said former surname of[4]
                      and on his [her] behalf assume adopt and determine to take
and use from the date hereof the surname of[3]   in substitution
for his [her] former surname of[4]

2   The said[3]   will at all times hereafter in all records deeds
documents and other writings and in all actions and proceedings as well as in all
dealings and transactions and on all occasions whatsoever use and subscribe the
said name of[3]   as his [her] surname in substitution for his [her]
former surname of[4]   so relinquished as aforesaid to the intent
that the said[7]   may hereafter be called known or
distinguished not by the former surname of   but by the
surname of   only.

3   I [we] on behalf of the said[3]   authorise and require all
persons at all times to designate describe and address the said   [7]
by the adopted surname of

IN WITNESS whereof I [we] have hereunto set my [our] hand and seal the day
and year first above written.

SIGNED AS A DEED AND DELIVERED
   by the said[8]

in the presence of[9]

---

[1]   Omit if not so: cf note 1 to Form 1 *above*.

[2] As to a person having parental responsibility making a deed changing a child's name, *see* p 94 et seq and generally Chapter 5.

[3] Full new name of child.

[4] Former name in full. If the deed is to be enrolled, the Central Office prefers 'formerly called . . .'

[5] Insert the child's age. *See* p 94 et seq and Form 7 *below* if child is 16 or over.

[6] *See* reg 2, p 90, striking out as necessary so as to leave standing the appropriate description of the child's citizenship. If the deed is not to be enrolled, no reference to citizenship is necessary.

[7] Name the child. If the child is male and already married, the words 'his wife and children' may be added. *See also* note 6 to Form 1.

[8] The person having parental responsibility should execute the deed in his own name.

[9] *See* note 10 to Form 1, reg 8(4) and pp 94–5. *See also* Forms 4 and 5.

Form 7: Consent by child over 16

(See p 94 et seq)

I,

of

being of the age of   years hereby certify that I have read and
approve the several matters witnessed and declared by the within-written Change
of Name Deed, and I hereby consent to the change of my name from
            to   as therein witnessed and to the enrolment of the
said Deed in the Central Office of the Supreme Court of Judicature.

(Signed)....................................

formerly known as

....

Witness ....

Form 8: Deed poll by local authority having parental responsibility on change of name of child in its care

THIS DEED dated the   day of   19   (which is intended to be enrolled in the Central Office of the Supreme Court) [1] made by THE   COUNTY COUNCIL on behalf of [2]
formerly called [3]   a child in our care and in respect of whom parental rights are vested in us pursuant to Section 31 of the Children Act 1989 [4].

WITNESSES

1   The said   is single a child of the age of   years and [a British citizen/a British Dependent Territories citizen/a British Overseas citizen/a Commonwealth citizen under section   of the British Nationality Act 1981] [5].

2   On behalf of the said [2]   we absolutely renounce relinquish and abandon the use of his/her said former [names] [surname] [6] of
                   and in substitution therefor on his/her behalf adopt and formally assume the [names] [surname] [6] of

3   On behalf of the said [2]   and with the intent that he/she will at all times hereafter be known or distinguished by the said [name/s] [surname] of   we declare that he/she will in all records deeds documents and other writings and in all actions and proceedings as well as in all dealings and transactions and for all other purposes (if any) and on all occasions use and subscribe only the [name/s] [surname   ] [2]   in lieu of his/her said former name/s and on his/her behalf we hereby authorise all persons to designate and address him/her accordingly.

IN WITNESS whereof we have executed these presents the day and year first before written

The Common Seal of
THE   COUNTY COUNCIL
was hereunto affixed in the presence of

---

[1]   Omit if not so intended.
[2]   New names in full.
[3]   Old names in full.
[4]   State appropriate section.
[5]   Strike out the inappropriate descriptions and insert the section number as necessary in order to comply with reg 2 (p 90 *above*).

6. Adapt according to whether the change is of surname only or of forenames as well, and *see* the appropriate form of additional wording for a change of Christian name at p 97.

Form 9: Affidavit supporting application for enrolment of deed poll where local authority has parental responsibility[1]

In the High Court of Justice

In the matter of a Deed Poll for change of name executed on behalf of [assumed name of child] (a child)

I [deponent] of [address] make oath and say as follows:

1 I am an [officer of the Social Services Department] of the [name of local authority] ('the Council') being a local authority in which is vested parental responsibility in respect of [assumed name of child] aged [age] by virtue of an Order of the   Court made [date] under the Children Act 1989, Section [31] and I am duly authorised by a resolution of the Council to make this affidavit and to submit this application on behalf of [assumed name of child][2]

2 I submit that the change of the said child's name/s as witnessed by the said Deed Poll now produced and shown to me and marked "   " is for the benefit of the child for the following reasons: [set out reasons]

SWORN etc   signature of deponent

---

[1] As to the meaning of parental responsibility *see* CA 1989, s 3; and for the acquisition of parental responsibility by a local authority *see* p 72.
[2] *See also Practice Direction* (1995) *The Times*, 17 February at Appendix B regarding additional consents.

Form 10: Statutory declaration as to identity

(*See also* Form 11)

I,[1]

of   [2]

do solemnly and sincerely declare as follows:

  1   I am a Commonwealth citizen and a householder residing at

  2   I have for[3]   years and upwards known[4]
formerly known as[5]   (who has executed the Deed now
produced and shown to me and marked 'A'), and whom I identify with the person
referred to in the documents exhibited to this Declaration.

  3   The Certificate of[6]   now produced and shown to me and
marked 'B' is the Certificate of[6]   of the said[4]
formerly known as   [5]

  4   I declare as aforesaid from my personal knowledge of the said[4]
          and of   said change of name and I make this
solemn Declaration conscientiously believing the same to be true and by virtue
of the provisions of the Statutory Declarations Act 1835.

DECLARED by the above-named ⎫

  at   ⎪
  this   ⎬
  day of   19   ⎪
    before me,   ⎭

          A Commissioner for Oaths.

---

[1] Must be a Commonwealth citizen who is a householder resident in the United Kingdom,
and should not be a near relation of the person changing his name. *See* reg 4, p 92.

[2] Insert address and occupation.

[3] Should not ordinarily be less than ten years: *see* reg 4, p 92, but the period may be shorter
(at the Master's discretion) in the young children's cases, in cases where the applicant
has changed his place of abode, or where there are other circumstances which render
strict compliance impracticable. *See* reg 8(6) which states that the householder must state
how long he has known the deponent and the child respectively.

[4] New name.

[5] Old name.

[6] This will be the Certificate of Birth, Citizenship or otherwise as appropriate under para
3(1) of the regulations. An applicant who is married must also produce the further
certificates or documents prescribed by *ibid*, para 3(2), in which case this Declaration
must be amplified accordingly (*see* Form 11).

Form 11: Statutory declaration as to identity—special cases[1]

(For use where applicant for enrolment of the Deed Poll in the Central Office is a parent, guardian or other person having parental responsibility, a married person, a widow or a feme sole; adaptable for 'Family Deed' cases.)

I,

of

do solemnly and sincerely declare as follows:

1   I am a Commonwealth citizen and a householder residing at
in the County of

[Parent, Guardian or other person having parental responsibility]
[2[2]   I have [for   years and upwards] [since [his] [her] birth] personally known and been well acquainted with[3]   (formerly known as[4]   ) the [child] whose change of name is evidenced by the Deed now produced and shown to me and marked 'A'; and I have also known and been well acquainted with[5]   for   years and upwards being the deponent to the Affidavit now produced and shown to me and marked 'B'.

All other cases]

[2[2]   I have for   years and upwards personally known and been well acquainted with[3]   [formerly known as[4]   ] the applicant for enrolment of the Deed now produced and shown to me and marked 'A'.]

[Parent or Guardian or other person having parental responsibility]
[3[2]   The Birth Certificate now produced and shown to me and marked 'B' is the Birth Certificate of the said[3]   formerly known as[4]
. The said Deed marked 'A' has been executed by[6]
having parental responsibility for the said child   . The child referred to as[4]   in the said Birth Certificate is one and the same person.

Married Person]
3[2]   The Certificate of [Birth] [Naturalisation] [Registration of Citizenship] and the Certificate of Marriage now produced and shown to me and marked respectively 'B' and 'C' are respectively the certificate of the [birth] [naturalisation] [citizenship] of the said[7]   and the certificate of the marriage of the said[7]   (formerly known as[4]   [and in the said certificates described as[8]   ]) with[9].
The said[7]   referred to in the aforesaid Deed Poll and in the said Certificate of [Birth] [Naturalisation] [Registration] and in the said Certificate of Marriage as[8]   is one and the same person.]

Widow]

[3[2] The Certificate of [Birth] [Naturalisation] [Registration of Citizenship] now produced and shown to me marked 'B' the Certificate of Marriage now produced and shown to me marked 'C' and the Death Certificate now produced and shown to me marked 'D' are respectively the certificate of the [birth] [citizenship] of the said[7]   the certificate of the marriage of the said[7]   (formerly known as[4] and in the said certificates described as[8]   ) with[10]   and the certificate of the death of the said[10]

The said[7]   referred to in the aforesaid Deed Poll and in the said Certificate of Marriage and in the said [Birth] [Naturalisation] Certificate as[8]   is one and the same person. The said[10] referred to in the said Certificate of Marriage and the said Death Certificate as[10] is one and the same person.

Feme Sole]

[3[2] The Certificate of [Birth] [Naturalisation] [Registration of Citizenship] now produced and shown to me marked 'B' the Certificate of Marriage now produced and shown to me marked 'C' and the certified copy decree absolute of the [   ] Court now produced and shown to me marked 'D' are respectively the certificate of the [birth] [naturalisation] [citizenship] of the said[7]   the certificate of the marriage of the said[7]   (formerly known as[4]   and in the said certificates described as[8]   ) with[10]   and a copy of a decree dissolving the same marriage. The said[7] referred to in the aforesaid Deed Poll and in the said Certificate of Marriage and in the said [Birth] [Naturalisation] Certificate as[8]   is one and the same person.]

For all cases]

4   I declare as aforesaid from my personal knowledge of the said[7] [and of the said[3]   and his/her parents] and of the said change of name of the said[11]   and I make this solemn Declaration conscientiously believing the same to be true and by virtue of the provisions of the Statutory Declarations Act 1835.

DECLARED etc

---

1 *See generally* the notes to Form 10.

2 Use whichever para 2 and whichever para 3 is applicable. Further adaptation of the 'Parent or Guardian' variants will be necessary if, exceptionally, the applicant is not a parent (*see* reg 8(5)(*a*)(iii), 8(6)). The 'widow' and 'feme sole' paragraphs will be necessary as a means of linking identities as required by reg 4, and possibly of establishing a particular citizenship.

3 New name of child/children in children and Family Deed cases.

[4]   Name now being relinquished.
[5]   The deponent under para 8(5)(*a*) of the 1994 Regulations.
[6]   The person with parental responsibility by whom the deed has actually been executed.
[7]   Applicant (new name).
[8]   In the case of a woman applicant insert her maiden or other name as stated in the certificate.
[9]   Spouse, naming him or her as in the certificate.
[10] Former husband, naming him as in the certificate.
[11] Applicant or child/children as the case may be.

Form 12: Suggested form of affidavit of 'best interest' in support of application for enrolment of Deed Poll evidencing change of name of child

(Reg 8(5)(*a*))

IN THE HIGH COURT OF JUSTICE

IN THE MATTER of an Application for Enrolment in the Central Office of a Deed Poll dated [date] and executed by [name of person having parental responsibility who executed the Deed] on behalf of [assumed name of child/children]

I,[1] [full name]
of [address]
make oath and say as follows:

[1.1 (adapt as necessary) I am the [father] [mother] [other person with parental responsibility stating how it was obtained] of/for [name of child/children][3] [state names and ages] the [child/children] named in the above-mentioned Deed Poll a copy of which is now shown to me and marked " " and which was executed by [state who executed the deed poll] on behalf of [myself] [my wife] [and] [our child/children] [state names and ages]] [[child/children] for whom I have parental responsibility]]

[1.2 The above-mentioned Deed Poll purports to evidence the change of [his] [her] [their] name[s] from[2]   to[3]

2 This application for enrolment of the said Deed is submitted by me [and by   the [mother] [father] [other person/s having parental responsibility] [of/for] the said child/children namely   [being the only other], [all other persons having parental responsibility for the said child/children

3[4] The consent of [mother] [father] [other person/s having parental responsibility] [being the only other person/all other person/s having parental responsibility for the said child/children] to the change of name is evidenced by [his] [her] [their] consent [endorsed upon the said Deed] [contained in the letter now produced and shown to me and marked " ", which I say [is in the usual handwriting] [is subscribed with the usual signature] of my [wife] [husband] [other person having parental responsibility] the child's said [mother] [father] [other person having parental responsibility stating how it was acquired]

3[4] I have been unable to obtain the consent of my [wife] [husband] [name of person having parental responsibility] the [mother] [father] [state relationship of other person having parental responsibility of the child/children and how it was acquired] of the said [child/children] because [he/she is dead/overseas], [although I have made every reasonable attempt to trace [him] [her], I have not succeeded in doing so.] (*Here set out fully the endeavours that have been made, exhibiting any correspondence sent and the replies, if any, received and indicate the time when the parent or other person with parental responsibility was last heard of and where, and whether any steps to obtain maintenance have been made. If it is known that the missing parent is living with another partner, state how long the association has lasted, and whether the partner has children, whether of the association or of any other person.*)

3[4] I have fully informed [name/s] the [father] [mother] [other person/s having parental responsibility] [of/for] the said child/children of the said Deed Poll and of its contents and that I intend to make this application for its enrolment. [He] [She] [Name of other person with parental responsibility] [has informed me that [he] [she] [objects] [does not consent] to the submission of this application for the reason that (*set out the reason given*).] [He] [She] has not replied to [any of my letters] [my request that [he] [she] consent to this application (*set out the efforts made to obtain a reply, exhibiting any correspondence*)].]

4 I submit that the change of the said [child's/children's] name[s] as witnessed by the said Deed Poll is for the benefit of the [child/children] for the following reasons:

[[4] I am the [father] [mother] [state relationship of other person having parental responsibility of the said child/children and [[here state circumstances eg [I and my wife and our other children have for   years and upwards been known by the name of[3]   ] or [have decided to adopt the name of[3]   ] [as is witnessed by the said Deed Poll] and it is desirable in the interests of the said child/children that [he] [she] [they] shall be associated in popular repute with us and be known by the said name]].

[[4] I have [re]married and the said child/children lives with me and with my [second] [present] husband Mr   . It is desirable in the interests of the child/children that [he] [she] should also be known by the name of[3]   . My [husband Mr   (who has parental responsibility)] is satisfied with the arrangements under which we are living and is content that the child should bear his name. His [their] [name/s of other persons having parental responsibility] consent is [endorsed on the Deed] [contained in the letter now produced and shown to me marked "   ", which I say is subscribed with his [her] [their] usual signature][5].

[[4] The child/children, having attained the age of   years, expressly desires that [he] [she] shall in future be known for formal purposes by the name of[3]   , that being the name by which [his] [her] friends neighbours and associates already refer to [him] [her]]

OR (*as the case may be*)

5 **I** accordingly apply for enrolment of the above mentioned Deed Poll.

SWORN etc

---

[1] Name, address and description of deponent and *see* reg 8(5)(*a*)(i)–(iii) as to who may submit the application for enrolment.

[2] Old name.

[3] New name.

[4] Use whichever of the optional clauses numbered 3 and 4 is appropriate to the circumstances, adapting and supplementing as necessary. Note reg 8(5)(*a*)(iii) that 'some other person whose name and capacity are given for the reasons set out in the affidavit may submit the application'.

[5] This sub-clause is appropriate when the child's mother makes the application. The Central Office may insist on the new husband's written consent. It is prudent to obtain the same if possible.

Form 13: Advertisement for *London Gazette* on change of name by Deed Poll enrolled in Central Office

NOTICE IS HEREBY GIVEN that by a Deed Poll dated , 19 , and
enrolled in the Supreme Court of Judicature on , 19 ,[1]
of
single/married/widowed/divorced,[2]
a Commonwealth/British/Dependent Territories/Overseas/citizen[3] abandoned
the surname of[4] and assumed the surname
of

Dated this day of 19
[solicitors for the said][5]

formerly

[6]

---

[1] New name in full.

[2] The advertisement should follow the deed in stating whether the applicant is single, married, widowed or divorced (*see* reg 2(2)).

[3] *See* reg 2 and make the appropriate deletions.

[4] Former surname in full.

[5] New signature; or 'Solicitors for the said . . . formerly . . .'

[6] Former signature.

Form 14: Advertisement for *London Gazette* on change of name of a child

NOTICE is hereby given that by a Deed Poll dated , 19 ,
and enrolled in the Supreme Court of Judicature on , 19 ,
as[1] persons/person having parental responsibility[2], on behalf of[3] a
child, single and a Commonwealth/British/Dependent Territories/Overseas/citizen[4]
abandoned the surname of[5] and assumed in lieu thereof the
surname of[3]

Dated this day of 19

(Signed)[6]
(Address)[7]

[Solicitors for the said][8]

---

[1] Name the parent, guardian, or other person having parental responsibility who is executing the deed.

[2] If the child is 16 or over, is female and is married, and he or she executes the deed, Form 11 should be used in place of this form.

[3] New name of child in full.

[4] *See* reg 2, p 90, and delete whichever is inappropriate.

[5] Former surname of child.

[6] Signature may be either personal, or by solicitor.

[7] To be filled in only if signed by solicitor.

[8] Delete words in square brackets if personal signature.

Form 15: Statutory declaration

[Statutory Declarations Act 1835, Schedule.]

I,   of [*address and occupation*], do solemnly and sincerely declare, that [*the form of words in Form 1 (Deed Poll) may be adapted*] and I make this solemn declaration conscientiously believing the same to be true, and by virtue of the provisions of the Statutory Declarations Act 1835.

DECLARED etc

Form 16: Advertisement of intention to use changed name

I, of [*address and occupation*], heretofore called and known by the name of
hereby give notice that I have renounced and abandoned the
name of   and that I have assumed and intend henceforth on all
occasions whatsoever and at all times to sign and use and to be called and known
by the name of   in lieu of and in substitution for my former
name of
Dated this   day of   19

[*New signature*]

formerly

[*Former signature*]

---

*Forms 1, 6, 10, 13, 14 and 15 in this Appendix are (save for the notes referring to the text
of the book) reproduced by kind permission of The Solicitors' Law Stationery Society
Limited. Copies of these forms are obtainable from Oyez Stationery Group plc. When
ordering please quote as follows:*

Form 1: Con. 18A
Form 6: Con. 18B
Form 10: Con. 18C
Form 13: Con. 18D
Form 14: Con. 18E
Form 15: Miscellaneous No 1

Appendix B

Practice Direction

Practice Direction (Child: Change of surname) (1995)
The Times, 17 February

Where a person with parental responsibility for a child applied to change the surname of a child under the age of 18, the application had to be supported by the written consent of every other person with parental responsibility.

The Senior Master of the Queen's Bench Division so stated in a *Practice Direction* issued with the approval of the Master of the Rolls on December 20, 1994.

1(a) Where a person had by any order of the High Court, county court or family proceedings court been given parental responsibility for a child and applied to the central office, filing department, for the enrolment of a deed poll to change the surname (family name) of such child who was under the age of 18 years (unless in the case of a female, she was married below that age), the application had to be supported by the production of the consent in writing of every other person having parental responsibility.

(b) In the absence of such consent, the application would be adjourned generally unless and until leave was given to change the surname of such child in the proceedings in which the said order was made and such leave was produced to the central office.

2(a) Where an application was made to the central office, filing department, by a person who had not been given parental responsibility of the child by any order of the High Court, county court or family proceedings court for the enrolment of a deed poll to change the surname of such child who was under the age of 18 years (unless in the case of a female, she was married below that age), leave of the court to enrol such deed would be granted if the consent in writing of every person having parental responsibility was produced or if the person (or, if more than one, persons) having parental responsibility was dead or overseas or despite the exercise of reasonable diligence it had not been possible to find him or her for other good reason.

(b) In cases of doubt the senior master or, in his absence, the practice master would refer the matter to the Master of the Rolls.

(c) In the absence of any of the conditions specified above the senior master or the Master of the Rolls, as the case might be, could refer the matter to the Official Solicitor for investigation and report.

3   The directions were issued with the approval of the Master of the Rolls.

4   *Practice Direction (Minor: Change of Surname)*   dated May 24, 1976 ([1977] 1 WLR 1065) was revoked.

This *Practice Direction* is reproduced with the kind permission of *The Times* Newspapers Ltd.

Appendix C

Countries Relevant to Commonwealth Citizenship

Part 1: Countries (including their dependencies) whose citizens are Commonwealth citizens within the British Nationality Act 1981, s 37, Sched 3

Antigua and Barbuda
Australia
The Bahamas
Bangladesh
Barbados
Belize
Botswana
Brunei
Canada
Cyprus
Dominica
Fiji
The Gambia
Ghana
Grenada
Guyana
India
Jamaica

Kenya
Kiribati
Lesotho
Malawi
Malaysia
Maldives
Malta
Mauritius
Namibia
Nauru
New Zealand
Nigeria
Pakistan
Papua New Guinea
St Christopher and
  Nevis
St Lucia

St Vincent and the
  Grenadines
Seychelles
Sierra Leone
Singapore
Solomon Islands
South Africa
Sri Lanka
Swaziland
Tanzania
Tonga
Trinidad and Tobago
Tuvalu
Uganda
Vanuatu
Western Samoa
Zambia
Zimbabwe

Part 2: British Dependent Territories within the British Nationality Act 1981, Sched 6

Anguilla
Bermuda
British Antarctic Territory
British Indian Ocean Territory
Cayman Islands
Falkland Islands and Dependencies
Gibraltar
Montserrat

Pitcairn, Henderson, Ducie and Oeno
  Islands
St Helena and Dependencies
The Sovereign Base Areas of Akrotiri
  and Dhekelia
Turks and Caicos Islands
Virgin Islands

Appendix D

Addresses and Fees

Useful addresses

The Court Service
Supreme Court Group
Filing and Record Department
Central Office
Room EP(C)A 1978, 07
Royal Courts of Justice
Strand
London WC2A 2LL

Tel: 0171–936 6528

Public Record Office
Chancery Lane
London WC2A 1LR

Tel: 0171–876 3444

Adopted Children Register
OPCS
Smedley House
Trafalgar Road
Southport
Merseyside PR8 2HH

Tel: 0151–471 4314

Fees

Statutory declaration

Declaration   £5
Exhibit   £2

Notary public

No fixed fee, but a minimum of £30.

College of Arms

Preparation and enrolment of deed poll—no standard fee, each application being dealt with on its own facts. However, the fee is likely to be in the region of £250.

Central Office of the Supreme Court
Filing and Record Department

Enrolment fee £10
Advertisement fee £42.25 + VAT

Index